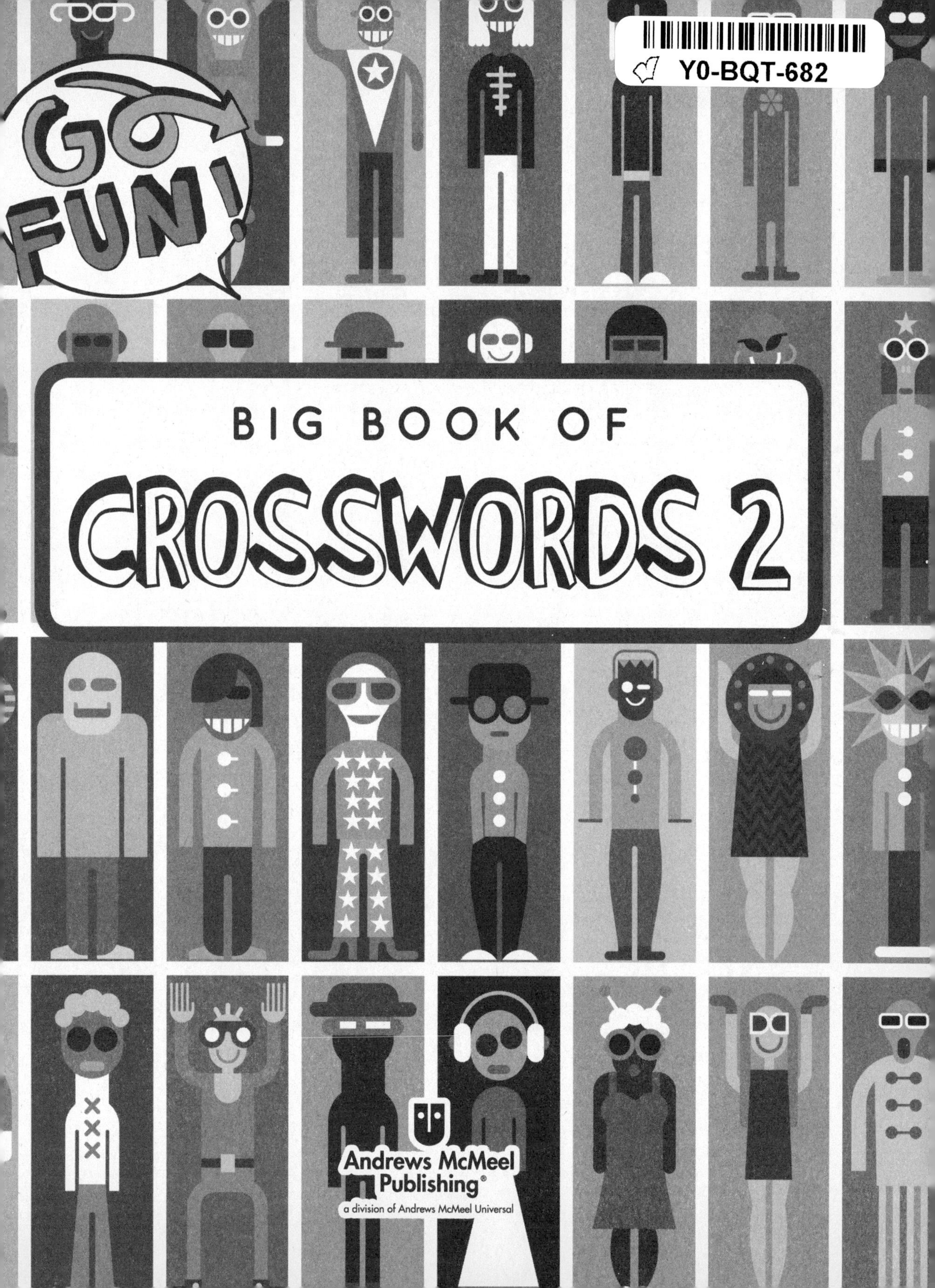
Y0-BQT-682
GO FUN!
BIG BOOK OF
CROSSWORDS 2
Andrews McMeel
Publishing®
a division of Andrews McMeel Universal

Andrews McMeel Publishing
a division of Andrews McMeel Universal
1130 Walnut Street, Kansas City, Missouri 64106

www.andrewsmcmeel.com

All puzzles supplied under license from Puzzler Media Ltd.
www.puzzler.com

16 17 18 19 20 PAH 10 9 8 7 6 5 4 3 2 1

ISBN: 978-1-4494-7882-7

Made by:
The P. A. Hutchison Company
Address and location of production:
400 Penn Avenue, Mayfield, PA 18433 USA
1st printing - 05/04/16

1

ACROSS

6 Direction or command (11)
7 Saying (6)
8 Male rabbit (4)
9 ____ Streep, actress (5)
11 Teacher (5)
13 Metal money (4)
15 Wild West character (6)
17 Difference, lack of agreement (11)

DOWN

1 Small measurement of length (4)
2 Constant (6)
3 Vast (4)
4 Thrust with a knife (4)
5 South American cloak (6)
10 Unusual, foreign (6)
12 Open a present (6)
14 Pleasant (4)
15 Crush with the teeth (4)
16 Cry of pain (4)

2

ACROSS

2 Swine (3)
5 Color of blood (3)
6 Kayak (5)
9 ____-hoop, round toy (4)
10 Move through water (4)
12 Rest on bended legs (5)
14 Honey-making insect (3)
15 Father (3)

DOWN

1 Ballpoint pen (4)
3 Farmyard birds (5)
4 Friend, mate (3)
6 Pool stick (3)
7 Nude (5)
8 Olive ____, golden liquid (3)
11 Spider's structure (3)
13 Close by (4)

3

Three to One

Each clue consists of three words, one of which is the correct answer. By comparing all the intersecting words, the full solution can be worked out. We have given you one answer to start you off.

1	■	2 D	■	3	■	4	■	5	6		7	
8		I						■		■		■
	■	A	■		■		■	9				
10		R						■		■		■
	■	Y	■		■		■	11				
■	12	■	13	■	14		15	■		■		■
16						■	17					
■		■		■	18	19		■		■		■
20					■		■	21	■	22	■	23
■		■		■	24							
25					■		■		■		■	
■		■		■	26							
27					■		■		■		■	

ACROSS

5 Aside • Chest • Stuck
8 Animator • Children • Primeval
9 Appal • Cream • Divan
10 Tarragon • Tortoise • Turnpike
11 Cause • Italy • Sport
14 Arm • Odd • Pet
16 Carpet • Manage • Pastel
17 Aspect • Office • Relics
18 Day • End • Gun
20 Charm • Fiery • Stork
24 Opposite • Sterling • Windmill
25 Bleak • Tonic • Wrath
26 Befallen • Ceilings • Geronimo
27 Adage • Bliss • Scuds

DOWN

1 Acute • Faith • Spite
2 Bread • Coded • ~~Diary~~
3 Corps • Nippy • Tempo
4 Banker • Hissed • Severe
6 Hornpipe • Suitable • Tomorrow
7 Classics • Deadlock • Shamrock
12 Catholic • Marigold • Pastoral
13 Fairways • Iterated • Sparring
14 Ate • Old • Peg
15 Dry • Mad • Ton
19 Apples • Netted • United
21 Brook • Coral • Oddly
22 Diana • Hilly • Mimic
23 Aglow • Least • Plank

4

Kriss Kross

See how quickly you can fit all the listed words into the interlocking grid.
We've filled in one word to start you off.

A S P I R E

3 Letters
AIM
ALE
JAR
LIE
NOT
RUM

4 Letters
EARL
NOON
SCAR
TAKE

5 Letters
CLASH
COMIC
GUEST
LODGE

6 Letters
~~ASPIRE~~
PLANET
RATING
SPRITE

7 Letters
BEDROOM
BEST MAN
CHEAPER
CRACKLE
EAGERLY
EMBARGO
LAUNDER
NEEDIER

8 Letters
ACCENTED
LAMINATE
MEANTIME
PAMPHLET
PRINCESS
UNBEATEN

9 Letters
ACCLAIMED
COMMUNITY
DALMATIAN
OCTAGONAL

5

ACROSS

1 Past of do (3)
3 Mail a letter (4)
5 North, South, ____, and West (4)
6 The ____ bitsy spider (4)
8 Maker of foam toys (4)
11 Noah's boat (3)
12 Synchronize, abbreviation (4)
15 Netting (4)
16 At any time (4)
17 Drop of liquid from your eye (4)
18 Had done (3)

DOWN

1 Opposite of up (4)
2 Word that starts a letter (4)
3 Smells bad (6)
4 Opposite of night (3)
7 Amaze, make speechless (4)
9 Slacken (4)
10 Male parent (6)
13 Unit of measurement, 36 inches long (4)
14 Ace, King, or 8 (6)
15 Object to wipe your shoes on (3)

6

ACROSS

1 Decorations on walls (6)
5 Clears mud from (a water channel) (7)
6 For (a charity) (2,3,2)
9 Dog's house (6)

DOWN

1 Spain's capital city (6)
2 Feel sorry (3)
3 Lump of firewood (3)
4 Handy (6)
7 Beer (3)
8 Lion's dwelling (3)

7

ACROSS

1 Out of danger (4)
3 Uses a spade (4)
7 Sprint (3)
8 Snow house (5)
9 Tin container (3)
10 Long, slippery fish (3)
12 Structure built by beavers (3)
14 Triceps and biceps (7)
15 Baby lion (3)
16 Travel across snow (3)
18 Very warm (3)
19 Disney deer (5)
21 Kanga's baby (3)
22 Swiss mountain range (4)
23 Seeing organs (4)

DOWN

1 Begin a game of tennis (5)
2 Society of supporters (3,4)
4 Unwell (3)
5 Heavy fall of rain or snow (5)
6 Disney film about a wooden puppet (9)
11 Large Australian bird (3)
12 Wreck, demolish (7)
13 Pose a question (3)
15 Hooded snake of India (5)
17 Removes creases from clothes (5)
20 Floor cleaner (3)

1		2		■	3	4		5
	■		■	6	■		■	
7			■	8				
	■	9			■	■	■	
10	11		■		■	12	13	
■	14							■
15			■		■	16		17
	■	■	■	18			■	
19		20			■	21		
	■		■		■		■	
22				■	23			

8

All Square

If you write the answers to these clues in the grid, you'll find that they read the same across and down.

1 Story
2 Large continent
3 Fibs
4 Simple

1				
2				
3				
4				

9

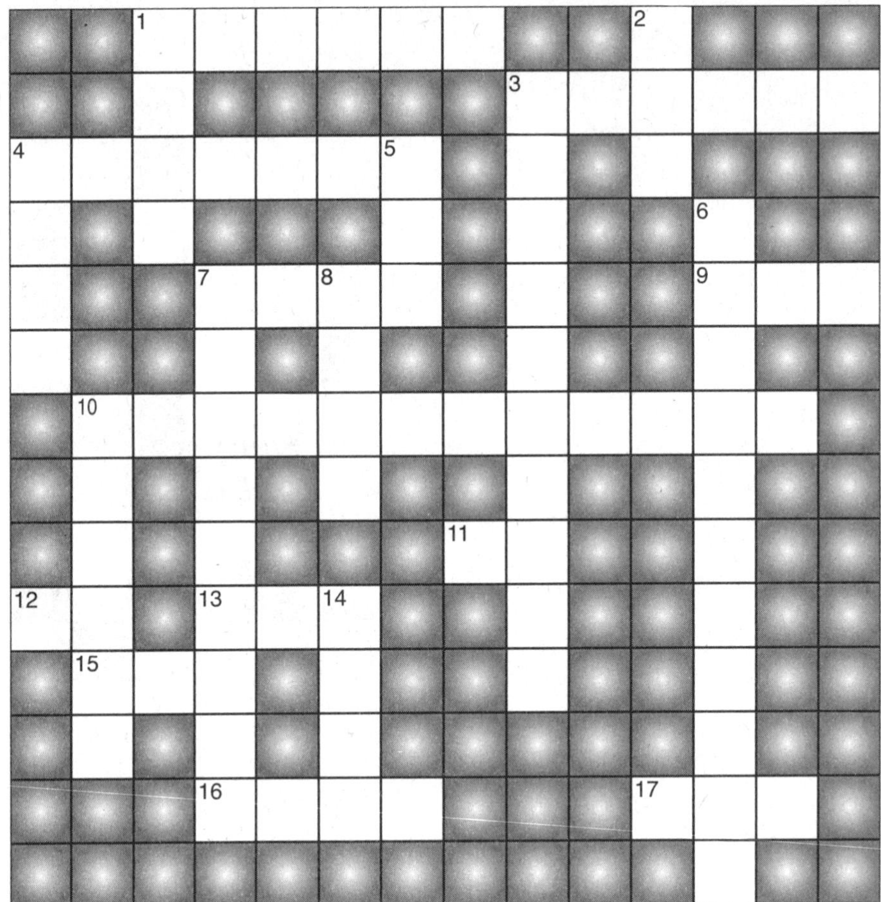

ACROSS

1 Rose, carnation, or lily
3 A message to a deity
4 One of the first group of people to celebrate 10 Across
7 ____ on the cob, maize dish
9 Headwear
10 Holiday in November
11 Opposite of down
12 Short version of okay
13 Consume food
15 Organ you listen with
16 Vegetables similar to sweet potatoes
17 At the moment, at this time

DOWN

1 Autumn season
2 Food for cows and horses
3 Popular dessert on 10 Across (7, 3)
4 Sweet, juicy fruit that becomes narrower toward the stem
5 Male human
6 Purpose of 10 Across (8, 3)
7 Small, red, sour-tasting berry served as a sauce with 10 Down
8 Gardening tool for sweeping leaves
10 Bird served at 10 Across
14 A group working together

Word Link

Starting at the top left, fit the names of the objects into the diagram so that the last letter of one word is the first letter of the next. But watch out, the pictures are not in order.

11

ACROSS

5 Large woody plant (4)
~~6 Press clothes (4)~~
7 Tip of a pen (3)
8 Place for baking (4)
9 Naked (4)
10 Woolen bedcover (7)
13 Farmed bird (7)
17 Not closed (4)
18 Very strong wind (4)
19 Fire remains (3)
20 Fifty-two weeks (4)
21 Not false (4)

DOWN

1 Courageous (5)
2 Small shelter for a dog (6)
3 Ape with very long arms (6)

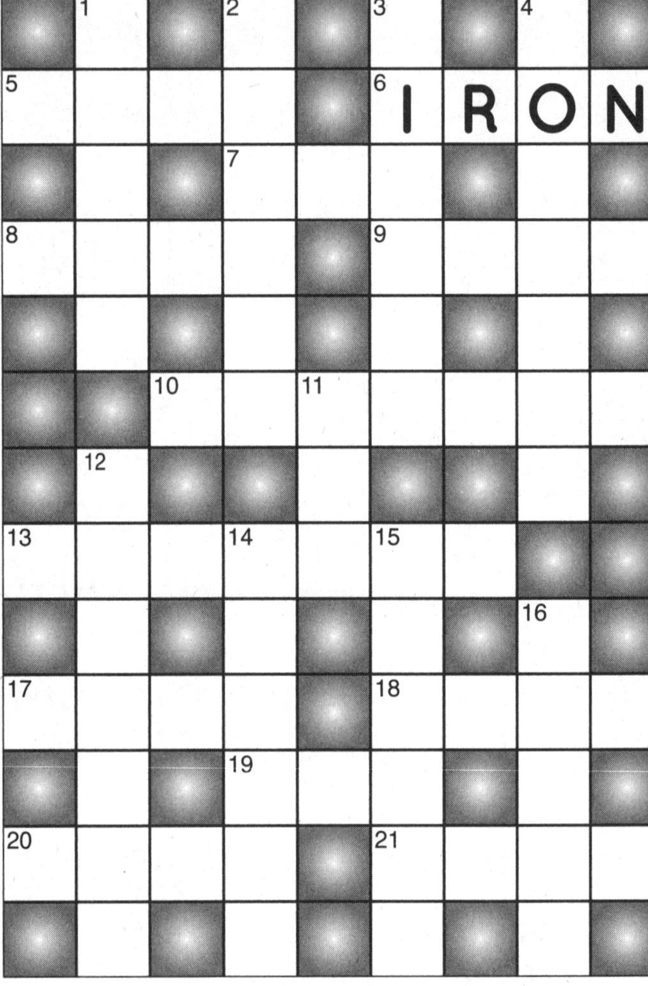

4 Voyage (7)
11 Noah's ship (3)
12 Section of a book (7)
14 Yellow singing bird (6)
15 Four times twenty (6)
16 Book of photos (5)

12

Kriss Kross

Fit the listed words in the grid. If you fill in the thirteen-letter word HIEROGLYPHICS that should help you to get started.

4 Letters
AMUN
BEER
GIZA
ISIS
LYRE
NILE

5 Letters
BOATS
EGYPT
GRAIN
HORUS
LINEN
LUXOR
STONE

6 Letters
AMULET
ANUBIS
BASTET

7 Letters
JEWELRY
OBELISK
PAPYRUS
PHARAOH
TEMPLES

8 Letters
PYRAMIDS

9 Letters
CLEOPATRA

11 Letters
TUTANKHAMUN

13 Letters
HIEROGLYPHICS

13

Code Cracker

In this puzzle, you must decide which letter of the alphabet is represented by each of the numbers from 1 to 26. We have already filled in two words, so you can see that T = 5, A = 12, I = 14, L = 7, and so on. Begin by repeating these letters in each box where their numbers appear in the diagram. You will then have lots of letters to help you start guessing at likely words in the grid. All the letters of the alphabet will be used, so as you decide what each one is, cross it off at the side of the grid and enter it into the reference grid at the bottom. The completed grid will look like a filled-in crossword.

A B C D E F G H I J K L M

3	6	5	26	12	■	10	■	22	3	26	23	■	1	■
18	■	24	■	23	■	12	6	3	■	■	12	5	11	17
20	2	14	9	11	26	2	■	5	3	25	5	■	22	■
12	■	3	■	15	■	21	3	5	■	24	■	1	3	5 T
5	11	13	13	3	3	■	■	7	■	11	4	3	26	12 A
11	■	■	3	■	12	9	24	3	■	26	■	3	■	14 I
26	3	4	12	14	26	■	12	■	4	3	5	26	11	7 L
■	16	■	25	■	7	12	25	3	26	■	26	■	14	■
8	3	2	5	7	21	■	5	■	14	9	14	9	7	3
12	■	3	■	3	■	23	3	12	19	■	12	■	■	12
7	7	12	17	12	■	3	■	■	3	9 C	7	12	14	26
3	12	5	■	26	■	5	3	12	■	24 H	■	7	■	19
■	21	■	8	2	12	5	■	8	7	12 A	9	14	3	26
10	3	26	11	■	■	3	21	3	■	11 O	■	22	■	20
■	26	■	19	11	11	26	■	19	■	25 S	5	3	12	17

N O P Q R S T U V W X Y Z

1	2	3	4	5	6	7	8	9	10	11	12	13
				T		L		C		O	A	

14	15	16	17	18	19	20	21	22	23	24	25	26
I										H	S	

14

Lost for Words

Some letters in this quotation from Albert Einstein have been left out, as well as all punctuation and word spaces. Can you fill in the missing letters to discover the full quotation?

N	O	T		V		R		T	H	I		G				T
C		N	B		C	O			T	E		C	O		N	T
	A		D	N	O			V	E		Y	T		I	N	G
	H	A	T			U	N	T	S		A	N			C	
U		T	E		.											

15

Rainbow Puzzle

Can you solve the seven clues? Each is an eight-letter word associated with a color. One letter of each is given to help you.

RED			R						French wine
ORANGE		A							Citrus fruit
YELLOW							I		Spring flower
GREEN			N						Unwanted plant
BLUE				B					Fruit of heathland shrub
INDIGO			O						Sprouting vegetable
VIOLET	W								Climbing shrub

16

Picture This

Write the name of each item pictured into the grid. If you do so correctly, the circled letters reading diagonally downward will spell out what this Boy Scout is going to be doing.

17

1		2		3	■	4		5
	■		■	6	7		■	
8			■	9				
	■	■	10	■		■	■	
11		12		13	■	14		
	■	15			■		■	
16			■	17				

ACROSS

1 Silky material (5)
4 Charge for work done (3)
6 Country north of Mexico (initials) (3)
8 ___fish, sushi (3)
9 Songs (5)
11 ___ up, confessed (5)
14 Use your eyes (3)
15 Single (3)
16 Conclusion (3)
17 Middle body part (5)

DOWN

1 Charles Dickens's Christmas miser (7)
2 Pull another vehicle (3)
3 Almond, for example (3)
4 Cooling device (3)
5 Simplest (7)
7 Nearest star (3)
10 Animal enclosure (3)
12 Move the head up and down (3)
13 Morning dampness (3)
14 Go downhill fast on snow (3)

18

Take Five

The answers to these clues are all five-letter words. Enter them into the grid, reading across, and the letters in the diagonal row should spell out a cold-sounding country.

1 Large gathering of people
2 Opposite of long
3 Playground item
4 Not moving
5 Frighten

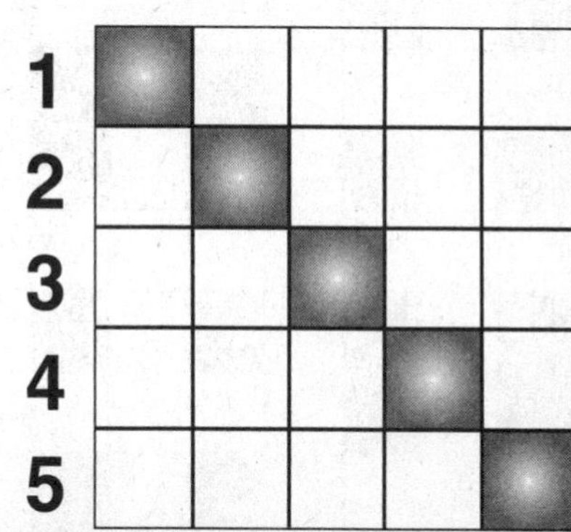

19

Arroword

Can you solve the puzzle? The arrows show you where to write your answers.

Riding mammal with hooves		Out and out, absolute		Gases in the atmos-phere	Snatch		Large farm birds
							Use your eyes
Small country house		Becomes weary					
Massive omnivo-rous mammal		Rub out, delete					
				Honey-making insect			

20

ACROSS

2 Regular payment (4)
4 Big boys' Japanese wrestling! (4)
5 Chair side (7)
6 School test (4)
7 Precious (4)

DOWN

1 The first light of day (7)
2 Fretter (7)
3 Loses one's sanity (4,3)

21

Kriss Kross

See how quickly you can fit all the listed words into the interlocking grid. We've filled in one word to start you off.

A D O R N

3 Letters
ACE
BEE
EFT
END
EWE
INK
MOP
VIM

4 Letters
AMEN
AREA
ARMY
BETA
EARL
ESPY
EVER
GIBE
KNEW
NEWT
PELT
RATE

5 Letters
~~ADORN~~
BRIDE
CREPE
DATED
GOING
GREEN
HEART
PALER
TIARA

6 Letters
BESIDE
CANDID
GRAINS
IMPACT
INTERN
LOCKET
STEREO
TAGGED

7 Letters
CABINET
CROSSLY
EARLIER
LACONIC
PELICAN
SKILLET
STAGGER
YEARNED

9 Letters
CHECKLIST
TALKATIVE
WHEATGERM

22

ACROSS

1 Product grown in fields by farmers (4)
4 A kind of tree, like oak (3)
5 Farm tool pulled by a tractor or cattle (4)
8 A place where crops and animals are raised (4)
9 Opposite of stand (3)
10 Shopping ____, item used to carry groceries (3)
12 Animal you can ride (5)
14 A long-necked bird that honks (5)

DOWN

1 A young male horse (4)
2 A baby dog (3)
3 Animal that gives milk (3)
6 A baby sheep (4)
7 Animals that chase mice (4)
8 An evergreen tree (3)
9 Fifth note in the musical scale (2)
11 Horned animal related to the sheep (4)
12 Another word for pig (3)
13 Organ we see with (3)

	1			2			3
4				5	6		
			7				
		8					
	9				10		11
12				13			
14							

23

Word Ladder

Can you climb down the word ladder from CUP to POT? Simply change one letter in CUP for the answer to the first clue, then one letter in that answer for the answer to the second clue, and so on.

CLUES

1 Little dog
2 Another name for dad

	C	U	P
1			
2			
	P	O	T

24

Picture This

Write the name of each item pictured into the grid, reading across. The circled letters will spell out the answer to the captain's question.

Abacus

Solve the clues and write the answers across the rows of white beads in the abacus. Then take out one letter from each row (shaded), reading downward but not in a straight line, to spell out a state.

1 Orange vegetable
2 Type of dance
3 Thick area of tropical forest
4 Frozen pudding (3,5)
5 Hot drink made from beans
6 Large rounded rock
7 Green precious stone
8 Disney's duck
9 Baby cat
10 Colored inflatable bag

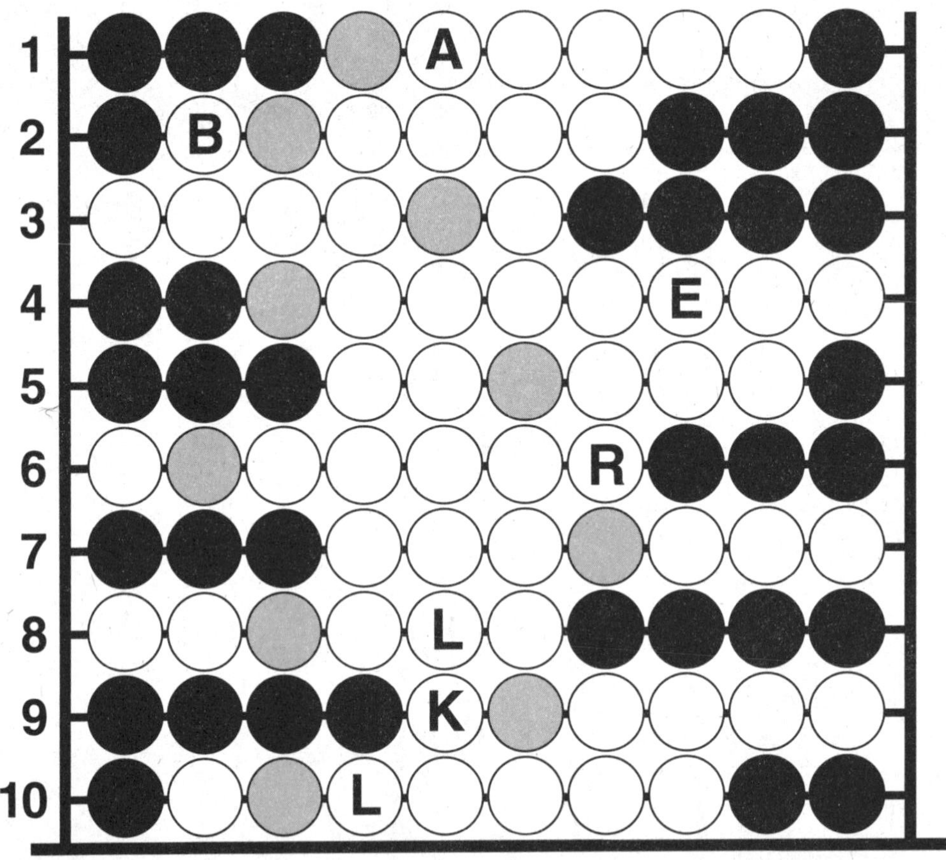

The state is: _ _ _ _ _ _ _ _ _ _

26

1		2		3		4
		5				
6				7		
		8				
9				10		

ACROSS

1 Stain material (3)
3 Crawling insect (3)
5 Pat softly (3)
6 Used a spade (3)
7 Not at home (3)
8 Flightless Australian bird (3)
9 I agree (3)
10 Black road-surfacing material

DOWN

1 ____ Warbucks, *Annie* character (5)
2 Borders (5)
3 Approximately (5)
4 Personal teacher (5)

27

Missing Letters

To solve the puzzle, write one letter in each of the boxes to make two six-letter words. Then transfer the new letters to the correct boxes below to spell out a period in history.

1	P R A I S	☐	M E R G E
2	G R O T T	☐	U T L A W
3	B O R I N	☐	R O U N D
4	R E V I S	☐	X P E R T
5	C A R E S	☐	C O R E D
6	C A R T O	☐	A T U R E
7	P H O B I	☐	C T U A L
8	C A R P E	☐	E A S E D

ANSWER BOX

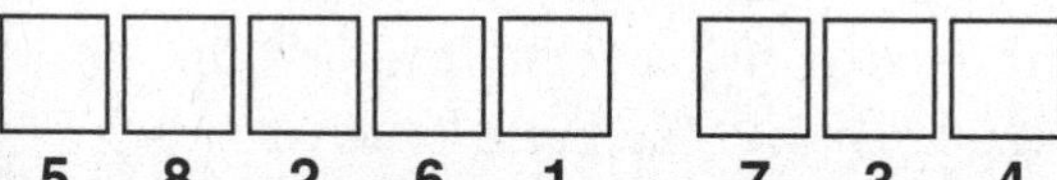

28

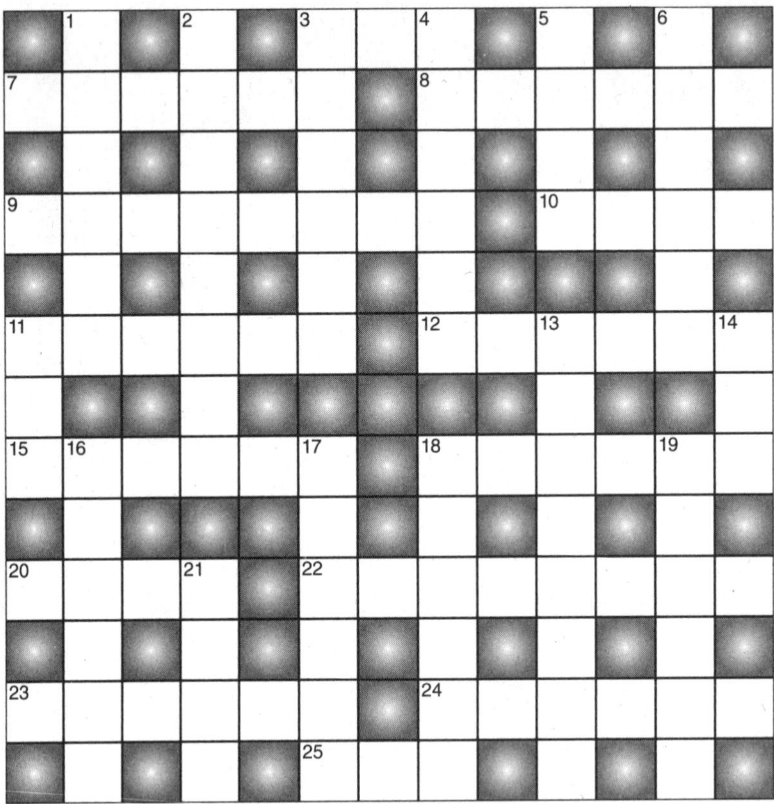

ACROSS

3 In good health (3)
7 Type of basket made from twigs (6)
8 Scared (6)
9 Unlucky number for some (8)
10 Twelve months (4)
11 Reach one's destination (6)
12 Show again (6)
15 Stockings (6)
18 Support for a broken limb (6)
20 Sightseeing journey (4)
22 Source of annoyance (8)
23 Permanent drawing on the skin (6)
24 Living things with roots, leaves, and stems (6)
25 Regret (3)

DOWN

1 To this place (6)
2 Affray, tussle (8)
3 Decorated band at the top of a wall (6)
4 Person who makes leather (6)
5 Predator's victim (4)
6 Insect remarkable for its loud chirping sound (6)
11 Suitable (3)
13 Very grand (of a building) (8)
14 Up until now (3)
16 Line drawn on a weather map (6)
17 Seaman, mariner (6)
18 Graze (6)
19 Number equal to ten times nine (6)
21 Habitual or mechanical routine or procedure (4)

29

Spiral Crossword

Every answer uses the last letter of the previous answer as its initial letter. The answers form a spiral to the center of the grid. The diagonals spell out two brass instruments.

1 ~~Industrial plant (7)~~
2 Fungus used in brewing (5)
3 Ping-pong (5,6)
4 Capital of Utah (4,4,4)
5 ____ University, Ivy League school in New Haven (4)
6 ____ Island, in Upper New York Bay (5)
7 Artist's workplace (6)
8 Meryl Streep film with Robert Redford (3,2,6)
9 Extraterrestrials (6)
10 Quickest route to somewhere (8)
11 Thin pieces of paper for blowing your nose (7)
12 There are sixty of these in a minute (7)
13 Opposite of rough (6)
14 National food of Scotland (6)
15 Places and things to see on vacation (6)
16 Buy things (4)
17 Small, round green vegetable (3)
18 Swiss mountain (3)

1 F		6			5				
A							10		
C				14					
T	7	11		17					
O						16	13		
R				18				9	
2 Y			15						
				12					4
	8								
	3								

30

Kitewords

In this puzzle, you must solve the clues and then fit the answers into the kite, reading across. We've filled in the first letters of the answers to help you decide where they fit, and the lengths of the answers should also give you a clue. If you do it correctly, the letters in the center column will spell out a breed of dog.

Attempt (3)
Honey maker (3)
____ space, where astronauts go (5)
Cost (5)
Tools for rubbing out pencil (7)
Country, capital Vienna (7)
Type of stick that always comes back to you (9)
Sons and ____, both kinds of children (9)
They repair horses' shoes (11)

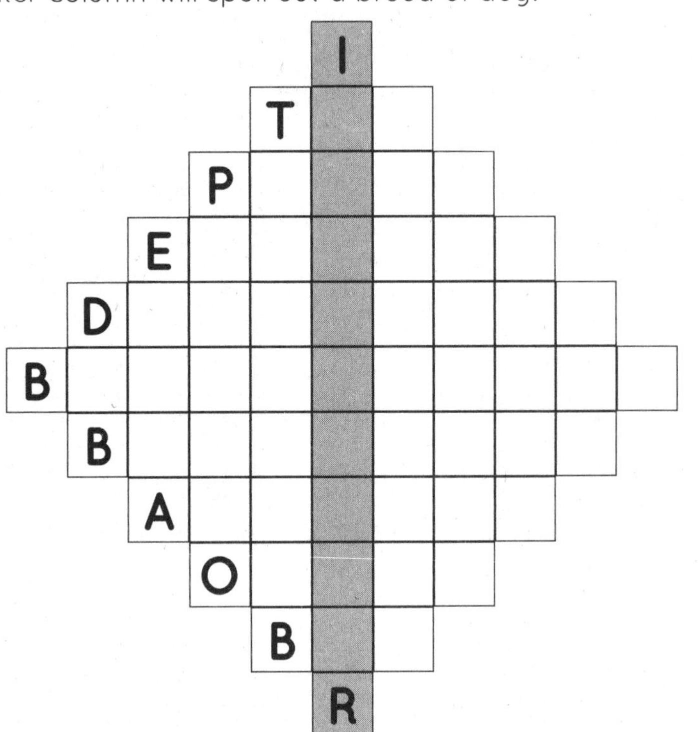

31

Word Ladder

Can you climb down the word ladder from PIE to HAT? Simply change one letter in PIE for the answer to the first clue, then one letter in that answer for the answer to the second clue, and so on.

CLUES
1 A deep hole
2 A light tap

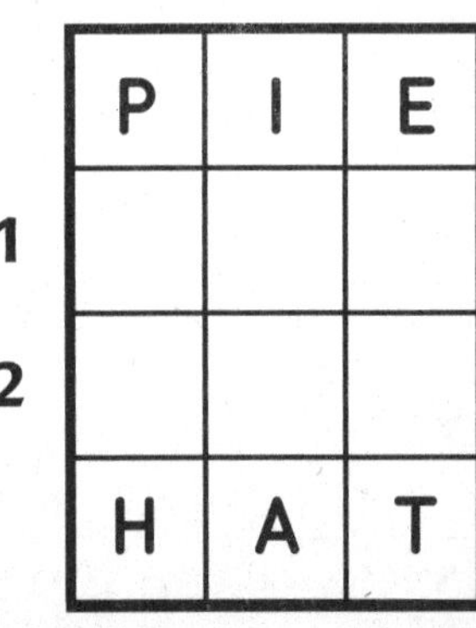

32

Leftover Letters

The answer to the clues in the two grids contain all the same letters, except for one. Write the extra letters from the first grid in the end column to find out the name of a famous basketball player.

1 A chess piece shaped like a horse's head • The period of darkness between sunset and sunrise
2 A yearly Christian holiday • Drops of water produced by the eye
3 Large cave, mostly underground • A large device for lifting and moving very heavy objects.
4 Recorded movies or programs • Birds of the pigeon family
5 Small house for a dog • To rest on the knees
6 A hot, dry, sandy region • Plants with woody trunks and branches
7 The son or daughter of an uncle or aunt • Metal money, cash
8 An attack of ____, a condition of being anxious • Number between six and eight
9 A radio or television antenna • Disney character, *The Little Mermaid*
10 ____ your seatbelts, get ready for take off • Any rich or large meal
11 A female parent • ____ Simpson, Marge's husband

1	K	N	I	G	H	T
2						
3						
4						
5						
6						
7						
8						
9						
10						
11						

N	I	G	H	T

K

This sign (•) separates the clues for the first and second grids.

33

Arroword

Can you solve the puzzle? The arrows show you where to write your answers.

__ Hood, Disney character		Spiritual creature with wings		Picture taken with a camera		Appliance for baking	Round, green edible seeds
				Jump on one leg			
The Earth's natural satellite		Covering for the hand					
				Earl Grey, for example			
Flames, heat, and smoke		Large maned cats					

34

Break Out

If you cross out any letter that appears more than once in the grid, the remaining letters will spell out a snack.

S	B	Q	L	A
B	N	B	D	U
W	T	V	M	L
Q	L	M	I	V
U	C	T	Q	H

35

Word Link

Starting at the top left, fit the names of the objects into the diagram so that the last letter of one word is the first letter of the next. But watch out, the pictures are not in order.

36

ACROSS

2 Baby's apron (3)
5 Movement of a tail (3)
6 What witches and wizards use (5)
9 Washtub (4)
10 Egg-shaped (4)
12 Possessor (5)
14 Function, purpose (3)
15 Knock gently (3)

DOWN

1 New Zealand bird (4)
3 Meaty breakfast food (5)
4 Feline animal (3)
6 Not woman (3)
7 Phantom (5)
8 Conflict between countries (3)
11 Animal doctor (3)
13 Not strong (4)

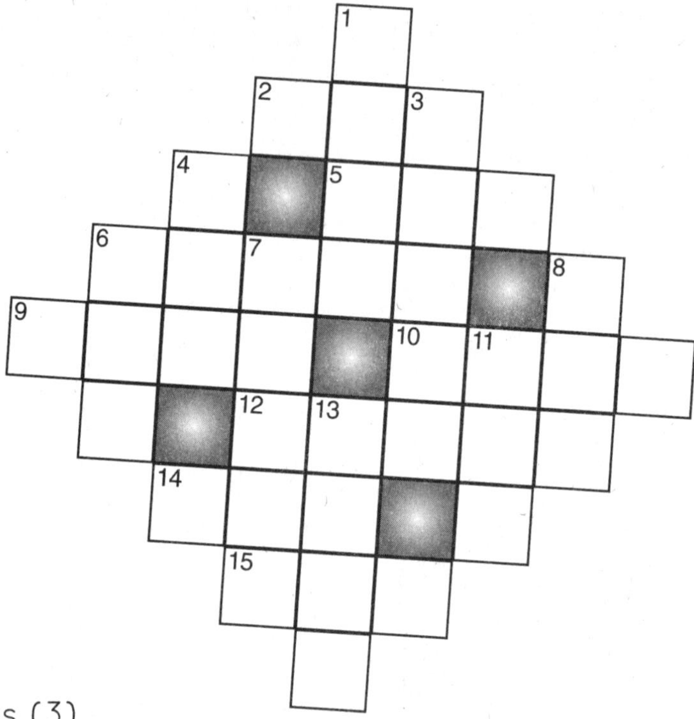

37

ACROSS

4 Flat vinyl disc with a groove for playing music (6)
5 Internet location (3,4)
8 Bad-mannered, rude (6)

DOWN

1 People that work on a boat or plane (4)
2 Impressions of prehistoric plants or animals in rock (7)
3 Make changes to something written (4)
6 Jealousy (4)
7 Hearing organs (4)

Rhyme Time

Fill in the missing vowels to complete the limerick.

39

It's a Fact!

The answers to these clues must be written across the rows of boxes in the grid. As you fill in the grid, transfer your letters to the coded boxes in the lower grid. If you do this correctly, you will reveal an interesting fact.

1 Piece of metal money
2 Found on the end of a finger
3 ___ Jonas, pop singer with the Jonas brothers
4 Tear-jerking vegetable
5 Letters, mail, etc.
6 Wise herb (anagram of gesa)
7 Smooth, shiny fabric
8 Actor's platform
9 Casserole
10 Me and ___, the two of us

1	1	2	3	4	
2	5	6	7	8	
3	9	10	11	12	
4	13	14	15	16	17
5	18	19	20	21	
6	22	23	24	25	
7	26	27	28	29	
8	30	31	32	33	34
9	35	36	37	38	
10	39	40	41		

23	4	■	13	29	6	18	3	’	26	■	31	2	5	24	41	25
27	20	■	30	19	■	28	40	9	33	■	10	36	■	1	32	14
8	7	11	12	■	15	21	35	■	16	38	17	■	34	39	37	22

40

Code Cracker

In this puzzle, you must decide which letter of the alphabet is represented by each of the numbers from 1 to 26. We have already filled in two words, so you can see that K = 7, I = 15, D = 13, and so on. Begin by repeating these letters in each box where their numbers appear in the diagram. You will then have lots of letters to help you start guessing at likely words in the grid. All the letters of the alphabet will be used, so as you decide what each one is, cross it off at the side of the grid and enter it into the reference grid at the bottom.

18	19	5	20	22	■	3	■	17	15	11	25	■	4	■
5	■	23	■	1	■	8	20	25	■	■	21	19	8	12
19	5	23	22	25	17	23	■	13	17	5	21	■	25	■
19	■	26	■	12	■	7 K	15 I	13 D	■	12	■	18	25	13
26	14	16	21	25	23	■	■	25	■	5	19	26	23	25
26	■	■	19	■	5	12	25	23	■	24	■	5	■	5
23	5	22	15	26	23	■	5	■	19	25	22 T	22	25	17
■	15	■	13	■	23	25	17	6	25	■	26 O	■	6	■
18	17	25	25	24	16	■	22	■	5	23	22 T	19	25	17
5	■	14	■	25	■	9	1	25	10	■	5 A	■	■	25
9	19	15	12	18	■	1	■	■	16	25	19 L	19	26	2
7	15	22	■	17	■	25	5	17	■	14	■	25	■	17
■	21	■	10	5	9	25	■	26	17	15	21	5	12	15
20	1	26	25	■	■	20	15	11	■	20	■	17	■	22
■	22	■	2	5	6	25	■	25	■	22	25	23	20	25

A B C D E F G H I J K L M

N O P Q R S T U V W X Y Z

1	2	3	4	5	6	7	8	9	10	11	12	13
				A		K						D

14	15	16	17	18	19	20	21	22	23	24	25	26
	I				L			T				O

41

Storyboard

If you write the answers to these clues in the grid, reading across, you'll find that the first column spells out the title of a book. If you transfer the letters from the grid to the table below, you will discover the name of the book's author.

1 Talking bird!
2 Flat, level
3 Red salad vegetable
4 Direction of sunrise
5 Hopping animal
6 Black-and-white colored bear
7 A door that is slightly open is ____
8 People next door

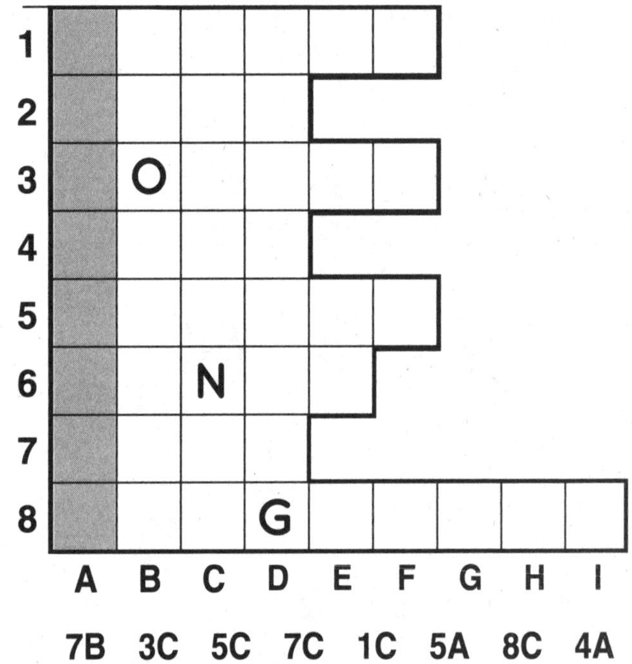

7B 3C 5C 7C 1C 5A 8C 4A

The author is:

42

Word Ladder

Can you climb down the word ladder from RED to TAN? Simply change one letter in RED for the answer to the first clue, then one letter in that answer for the answer to the second clue, and so on.

CLUES

1 A boy's name
2 The number after nine

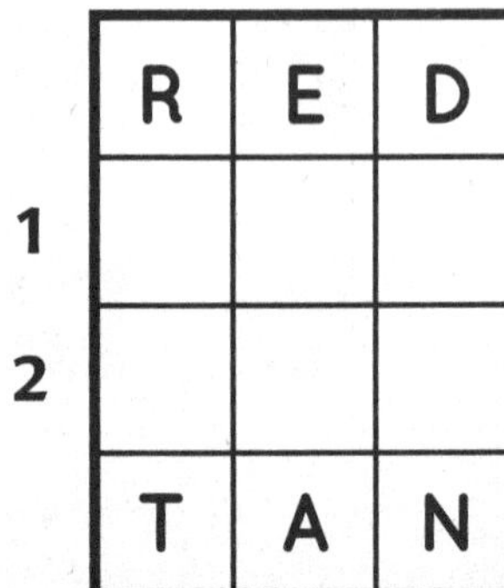

43

Picture This

Write the name of each item pictured into the grid, and the circled letters will spell out the missing ingredient the witch needs to complete her magic potion.

44

Word Ladder

Fill in each step with a genuine word, changing one letter at a time as you climb down from the top word to the bottom one. We've clued the steps for each ladder, but not in the correct order.

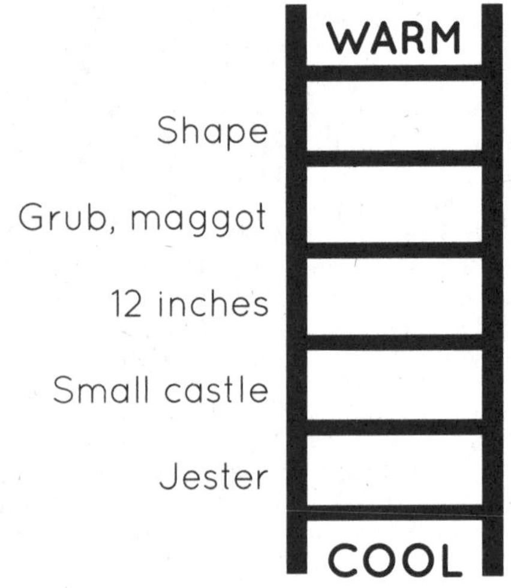

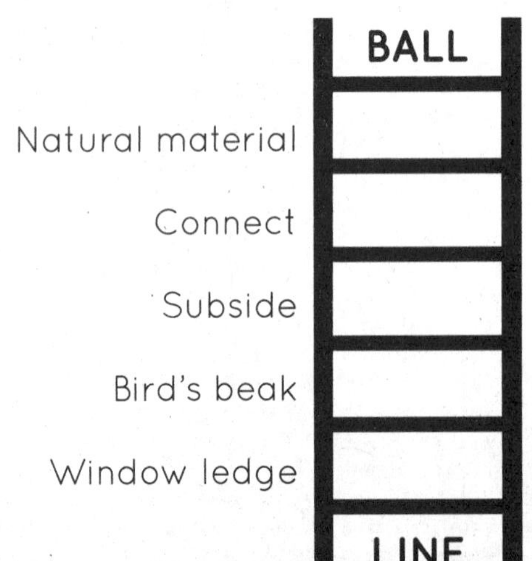

45

Fan-tas-tic

Solve the clues and enter your answers in the grid. Read the letters in the shaded circles from top to bottom to find a new word.

Shaded clue: Publication

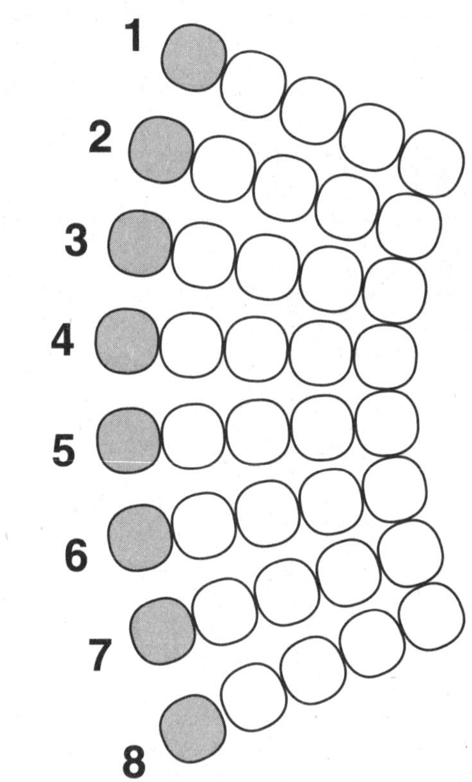

1 Exotic orange-fleshed fruit
2 Blacksmith's workbench
3 Cow's food
4 Bow's ammunition
5 Striped animal
6 List of contents
7 Sibling's daughter
8 Mistake

46

ACROSS

5 Number of digits on one hand (4)
6 Dull pain (4)
7 Everything (3)
8 Sound made by a snake (4)
9 Uncle's wife (4)
10 Very old (7)
13 Large cushion filled with polystyrene balls (7)
17 Compact ___, music device (4)
18 Go yachting (4)
19 Neckwear (3)
20 Molten stream from a volcano (4)
21 Short letter (4)

DOWN

1 Pay a call on somebody (5)
2 Winter or spring, for example (6)
3 Spicy Italian sausage (6)
4 Gleaming (7)
11 Male swan (3)
12 Water bird with large, pouched beak (7)
14 Sweet liquid sought by bees (6)
15 Away, not present (6)
16 Years in half a century (5)

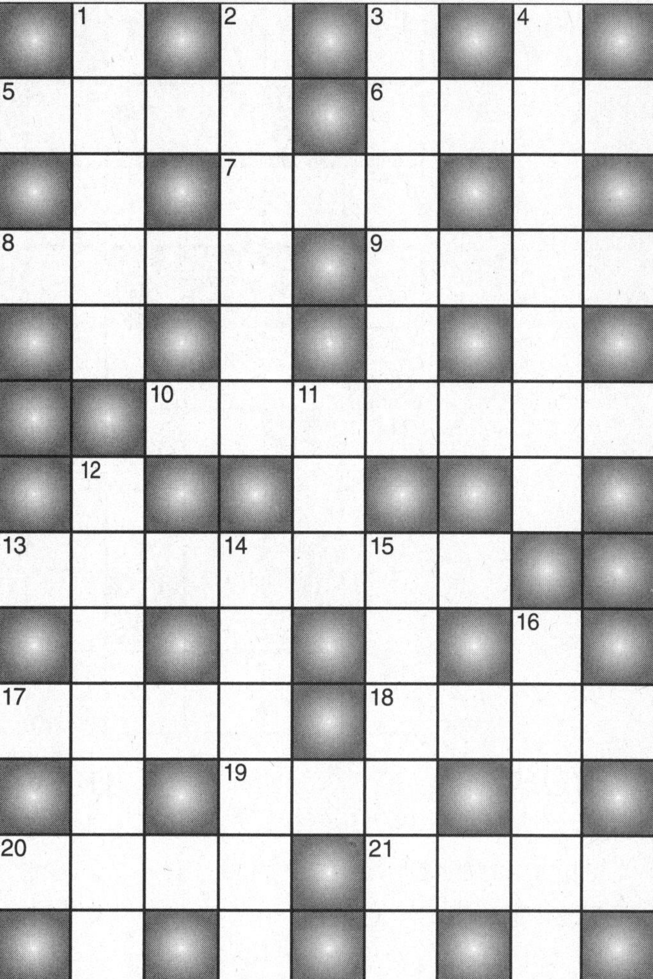

47

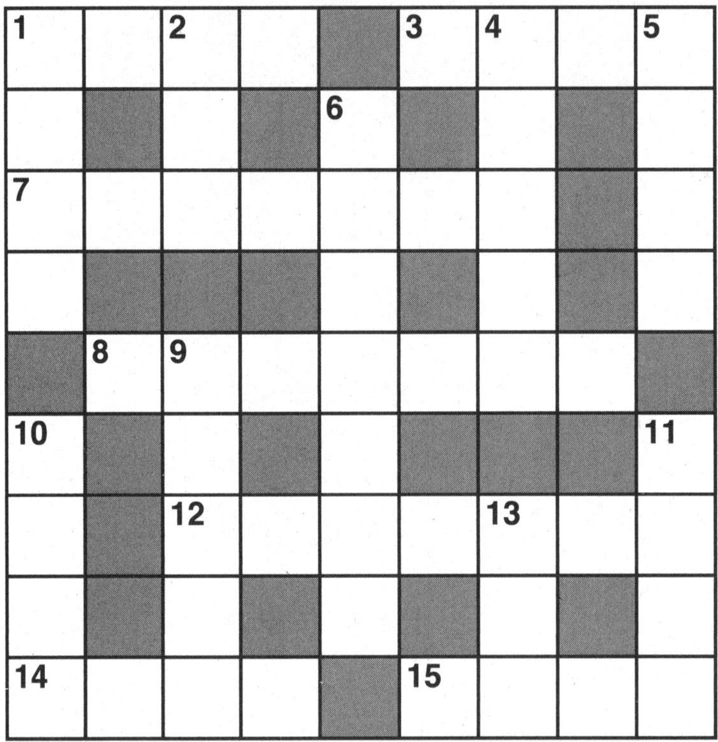

ACROSS

1 A flexible tube for carrying a liquid, such as water, to a desired point (4)

3 Mark left by a wound (4)

7 A portable case for enclosing a light and protecting it from the weather (7)

8 Person watching for something to happen (7)

12 Performer of gymnastic feats, perhaps in a circus (7)

14 Large grass-eating animal with antlers (4)

15 Mix with a spoon (4)

DOWN

1 Command for "stop marching" (4)

2 Bright burning disc in the sky (3)

4 Small, light, narrow boat, pointed at both ends (5)

5 Garden tool used for collecting leaves (4)

6 Written messages from one person to another (7)

9 Winged vehicle designed for air travel (5)

10 Credit ____, item used as a method of payment (4)

11 Very large ball of burning gas in space that is usually seen from the earth (4)

13 Small portion (3)

48

Change-a-Letter

Solve the clues below, changing one letter of your answer at a time. When you get to clue 12, you'll find that its answer is also one letter different from the first answer, WIDE.

1 ~~Broad~~
2 Walk through water
3 Sea feature
4 Rouse from sleep
5 Cook in the oven
6 Sponge or chocolate gateau, for example
7 Item of luggage
8 Bills and coins
9 Creamed potatoes
10 Remove dirt
11 Desire for something, expressed when blowing out birthday candles
12 Clever, like an owl

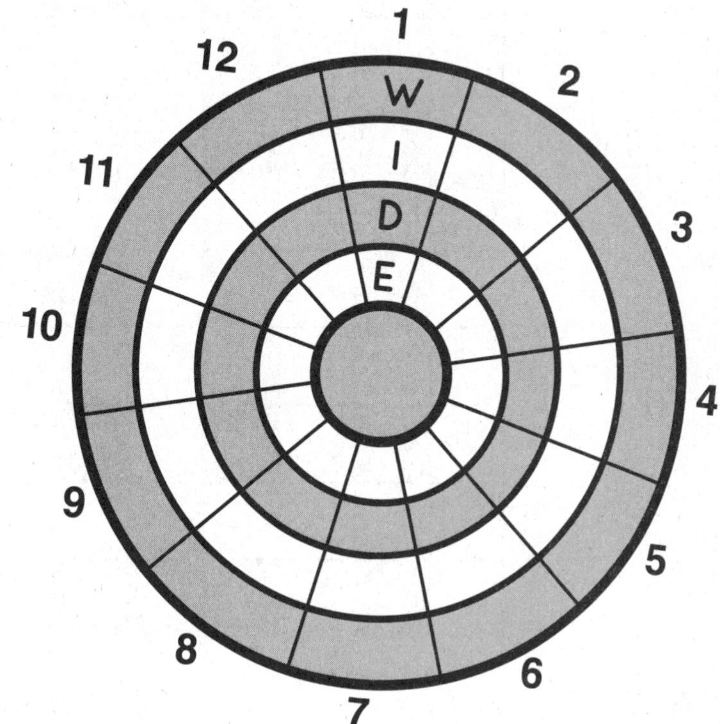

49

Word Ladder

Can you climb down the word ladder from BOY to MAN? Simply change one letter in BOY for the answer to the first clue, then one letter in that answer for the answer to the second clue, and so on.

CLUES

1 An inlet where boats dock
2 Month in spring

	B	O	Y
1			
2			
3	M	A	N

50

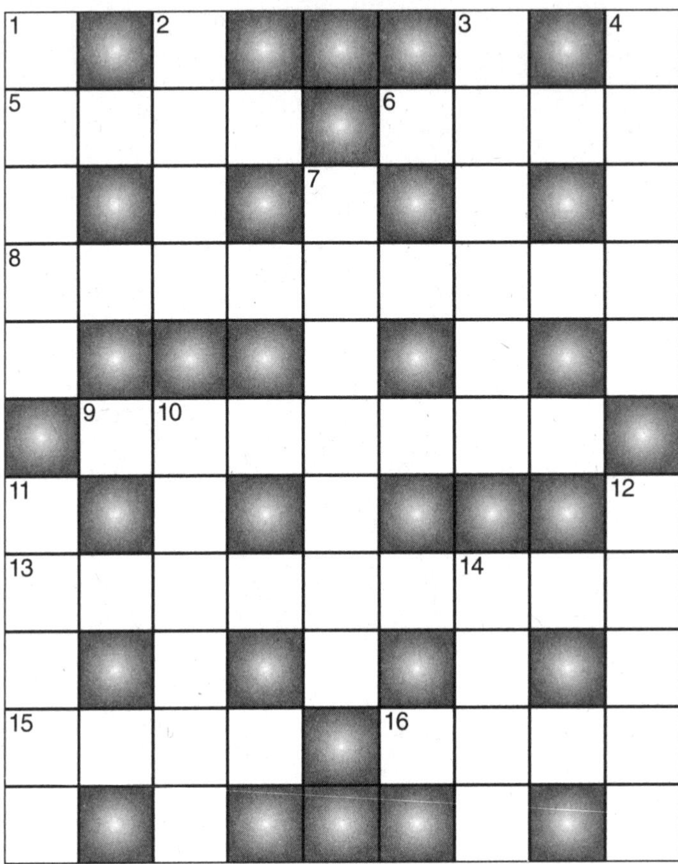

ACROSS

5 Tool for removing creases from clothes (4)

6 Having no hair (4)

8 Fierce destructive windstorm (9)

9 Person who delivers letters (7)

13 ____ *Gadget*, cartoon series (9)

15 Vegetable and symbol of Wales (4)

16 Yellow-and-black stinging insect (4)

DOWN

1 Number of tentacles on an octopus (5)

2 Sixty minutes (4)

3 Massive desert of northern Africa (6)

4 Britain's only venomous snake (5)

7 Four times four (7)

10 Shellfish that produces pearls (6)

11 Name of a book or film (5)

12 Fruit used in making wine (5)

14 Creature similar to a frog (4)

51

Holiday Time

Ben, Liz, and Ian are each going on holiday. To solve where they are going, follow the trails and write the letters in the boxes below.

52

Arroword

Can you solve the puzzle? The arrows show you where to write your answers.

Sports trainer		Flashlight		Wicked, heartless		Rhymes	
				Metal source		Water faucet	
Toy that spins up and down		Course of a journey					
Frozen dessert		Aids, assissts					

53

ACROSS

2 Spider traps (4)
4 Of the kind described (4)
5 Thought (4)
6 Top sound reproduction (2-2)
7 Accepted standard or a way of behaving or doing things (4)
8 Piece of cloth that represents a country (4)

DOWN

1 Relating to a marriage or to the state of being married (7)
2 Spending (time) pleasantly (7)
3 Beer producers (7)

54

ACROSS

1 To question (3)
2 Pink cooked meat from a pig (3)
5 Shapes with four sides (7)
6 Part of a bird's plumage (7)
8 Stir, combine ingredients (3)
9 Powerful aircraft (3)

DOWN

1 Really long time (4)
3 Disorder, confusion (4)
4 Talk rapidly (7)
6 Story seen in a cinema (4)
7 Boat made of logs (4)

55

Jigsaw

Can you fit the jigsaw pieces correctly into the grid, using the letters to help you spell out six different Christmas tree ornaments reading across the rows? One of the words is ICICLE. We've put some letters in to help get you started.

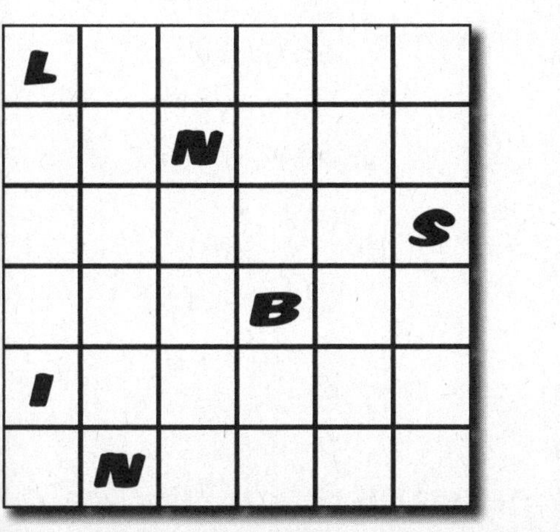

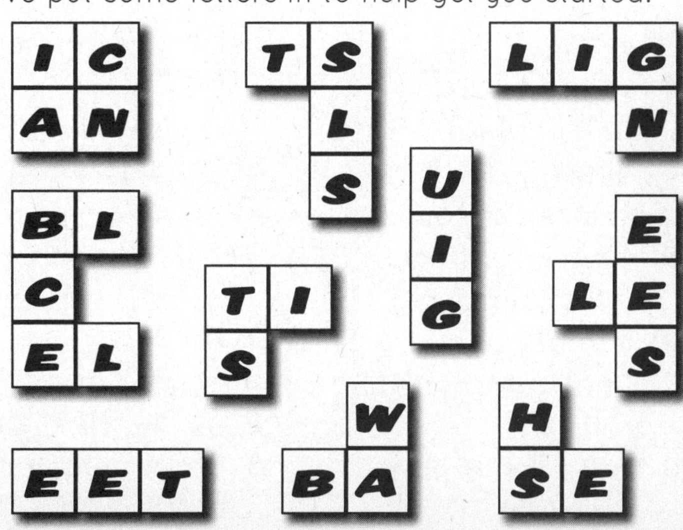

56

ACROSS

1 A conjurer does tricks like pulling a rabbit out of a hat by using ____ (5)
4 Grilled sliced bread (5)
7 *Peter ____*, children's story (3)
8 Move your head to show approval (3)
9 Animal's shelter (3)
10 Small green citrus fruit (4)
11 Tool for digging earth (5)
14 Pacific ____, large body of water (5)
16 Close with a key (4)
18 Lion's foot (3)
20 Sprint, hurry, go fast (3)
21 Organ of sight (3)
22 Move to music (5)
23 Holiday accommodation (5)

DOWN

1 Atlas pictures (4)
2 Authentic, real (7)
3 Small boat propelled by a paddle (5)
4 Movements of the sea (5)
5 Opposite of subtract (3)
6 Underground passage (6)
12 Very, very old (7)
13 Jumped on one leg (6)
15 Hospital worker (5)
16 Midday meal (5)
17 Back of the foot (4)
19 Be the first (to finish a race) (3)

Kriss Kross

Can you fit all the indoor games in the grid? To start, try to work out where the six-letter word, CLUEDO, must fit. Then you should be able to fit the others. When you've finished, write down the letters in the shaded squares to spell another indoor game.

4 Letters
LUDO

5 Letters
DARTS
JENGA

6 Letters
CLUEDO

8 Letters
CRIBBAGE
DRAUGHTS
SKITTLES

9 Letters
BAGATELLE
SOLITAIRE

10 Letters
BATTLESHIP
PICTIONARY

11 Letters
HIDE AND SEEK
TIDDLYWINKS

The other indoor game is _ _ _ _ _ _ _ _ !

58

ACROSS

1 *The* _____, Whitney Houston film (9)
5 Long bench in a church (3)
7 Shaded area caused by the sun shining on something (6)
8 Lava used as a cleaning stone (6)
10 List of meals (4)
11 Sea-fish of cod family (7)
13 Sport with swords (7)
17 Scared (7)
19 Image of a saint (4)
21 Useful tool (6)
22 Arab chieftain (6)
23 Knot (3)
24 Risky (9)

DOWN

1 Hit or thump (4)
2 Baby's nappy (6)
3 Drop of liquid (7)
4 Pagan priest of ancient Britain (5)
5 Jail (6)
6 Remnants of a crash (8)
9 Laugh quietly (7)
12 Battle between two or more people or groups using weapons that fire bullets (8)
14 Not either (7)
15 Short, broad-bladed oar (6)
16 Spotted game piece (6)
18 Newly made (5)
20 So (4)

59

ACROSS

1 Use a chair (3)
3 Star that gives us heat (3)
5 Sure, positive (7)
6 Go into a room (5)
9 Badly behaved (7)
10 Large area of water (3)
11 Food with a crust (3)

DOWN

1 Santas' bag (4)
2 Large hairy spider (9)
3 Vehicle for visiting the moon (9)
4 Zero (4)
7 Finishes (4)
8 Use a keyboard (4)

1		2		3		4
5						
	6					
7						8
9						
10				11		

60

Break Out

Sam has forgotten to pack an important item in her schoolbag. If you cross out any letter that appears more than once in the grid, the remaining letters will reveal what she has forgotten.

O	G	L	F	Y
F	S	M	U	B
K	N	B	P	S
L	P	U	I	O
O	T	F	N	L

61

Arroword

Write the answers to the clues starting in the squares shown by the arrows.

Word paired with neither	Court-room promise	↓	Part of a circle	↓	Kitchen or lounge, e.g.	↓	Run after
↳	↓		Animal, rodent		Passenger vehicle		Hot drink
Circus gymnast →			↓		↓		↓
Close or closed		Entertain →					
↳				Large body of salt water →			

62

ACROSS

4 Something mysterious that seems impossible to understand completely (6)

5 Medley (7)

8 ____ out, supplied someone with the clothes needed for a purpose (6)

DOWN

1 Tightly curled hairstyle (4)

2 Stir (7)

3 Beast's resting place (4)

6 Printing fluids (4)

7 Finishes (4)

63

ACROSS

1 Take as one's own child (5)
4 Start (5)
7 Divide in two (5)
9 Aladdin's friend who lives in a lamp (5)
10 Metal pin, bolt (5)
11 Wash out with water (5)
12 Big (5)
15 Score, account (5)
18 Chop (3)
20 Break out of prison (6)
21 Sudden, unexpected (6)
22 _____ Hatter, Lewis Carroll character (3)
24 Go into (5)
27 Travel by bike (5)
30 Dark-brown pigment (5)
31 Instrument section in an orchestra or band (5)
32 Subsequently (5)
33 Cards used in fortune-telling (5)
34 Funny (5)
35 Anesthetic gas (5)

DOWN

1 Heavenly being, often depicted with wings (5)
2 Person who possesses something (5)
3 In that place (5)
4 French headgear (5)
5 Judge's hammer (5)
6 Dapper, spruce (5)
8 Jouster's weapon (5)
13 Malicious fire-raising (5)
14 Part of a fireplace (5)
16 Imposing display (5)
17 Extended collar of a jacket (5)
18 Garment's sewn border (3)
19 Roll of bank notes (3)
23 Yellowish fossil resin (5)
24 Arm joint (5)
25 Grilled bread (5)
26 Corroded (5)
27 Tea chest (5)
28 Nab (5)
29 Mistake (5)

64

It's a Fact!

The answers to these clues must be written across the rows of boxes in the grid. As you fill in the grid, transfer your letters to the coded boxes in the lower grid. If you do this correctly, you will reveal a prehistoric pun.

A Barney ____, Fred Flintstone's pal (6)
B ____ van Gogh, famous painter (7)
C ____ Shakespeare, famous playwright (7)
D Type of owl found in Britain (5)
E The Mad ____, *Alice's Adventures in Wonderland* character (6)
F Make a noise like an owl (4)
G Sixty minutes (4)
H Trusty ____, reliable horse (5)
I To clean with liquid (4)
J Follow an animal by looking at its trail (5)

	1	2	3	4	5	6	7
A							
B							
C							
D							
E							
F							
G							
H							
I							
J							

C1	G1	D5	■	D3	C6	H1	■	E4	I4	B5	■	E6	G2	B4	J5	■
A4	A1	E2	B1	H3	G4	■	D1	E1	I2	B3	■	F4	F1	A6	■	C7
F2	G3	B6	E3	J3	B2	D4	?	C2	H2	■	I1	J3	I3	■	D2	■
A5	C5	J1	B7	C3	H4	■	A3	F3	A2	C4	H5	E5	J2	!		

65

Picture This

Write the name of each item pictured into the grid, and the circled letters will spell out the answer to the question.

66

Word Link

Starting at the top left, fit the names of the objects into the diagram so that the last letter of one word is the first letter of the next. But watch out, the pictures are not in order.

67

Arroword

Write the answers to the clues starting in the squares shown by the arrows.

__ Hood, Disney character	↴	Nocturnal flying mammal	↴	Device to catch an animal	Greases	Make less difficult	Hole for a coin
↳				↓	↓	↓	↓
Edible root veggies		Court case	→				
↳			Too, as well	→			
Sweet filled pastry		Troubled, worried	→				

68

Word Ladder

Can you climb down the word ladder from NONE to LOTS? Simply change one letter in NONE for the answer to the first clue, then one letter in that answer for the answer to the second clue, and so on.

CLUES

1 Ice cream cornet
2 Walking stick
3 Food tins
4 Furry feline pets
5 Camp beds

	N	O	N	E
1				
2				
3				
4				
5				
	L	O	T	S

Kriss Kross

Can you fit all the Christmas foods into the kriss kross? When you're done, rearrange the letters in the shadowed squares to spell out the answer to the joke below.

What two countries should the chef use when he's making Christmas dinner?

4 Letters

CAKE
DUCK
NUTS
PATE

5 Letters

BACON
CREAM
GOOSE
GRAVY

6 Letters

CHEESE
SALMON
TRIFLE

8 Letters

CRACKERS
PARSNIPS
POTATOES
SAUSAGES

ANSWER: _ _ _ _ _ _ _ and _ _ _ _ _ _ _ _!

70

ACROSS

1 Large group of people (5)
6 Snake that's good at math! (5)
7 Underwater explorer (5)
8 Cried (4)
0 Curved building structure (4)
3 Green citrus fruits (5)
4 Two times (5)
5 Stinging insects (5)

DOWN

2 Lift up (5)
3 Gloomy (4)
4 Where milk comes from in a cow (5)
5 Rubbish (5)
8 Without color (5)
9 Capital of France (5)
11 Low in price (5)
12 Traveled by airplane (4)

71

Egg Timer

To answer these clues you have to remove a letter from the previous answer and (if necessary) rearrange the letters to get the new answer. When you pass clue 5, you have to do the opposite—add a letter each time. We have put the first answer in to start you off.

~~1 Uncomfortably low temperature~~
2 More aged
3 Traveled by horse
4 Fisherman's stick
5 For better ____ worse (part of a wedding vow)
6 Line (of cabbages)
7 ____ away, eroded
8 Not as good as
9 Short burst of rain

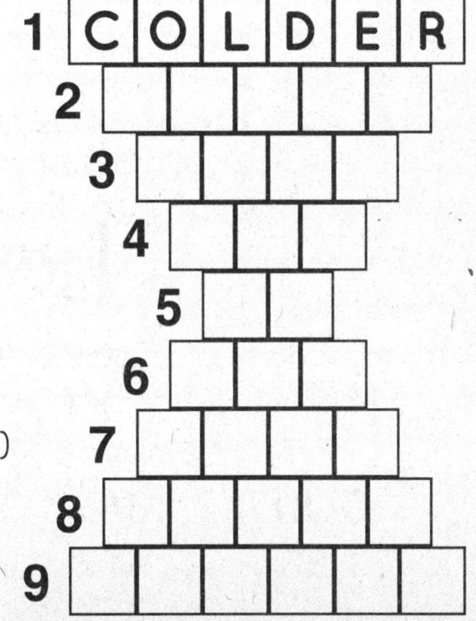

72

1		2			3	4		5
				6				
7								
	8	9						
10								11
		12				13		
14					15			

ACROSS

1 Opposite of easy (4)
3 Yellow grains on a beach (4)
7 Top-ranking soldier (7)
8 Period of gathering crops (7)
12 Large amount of money (7)
14 High in stature (4)
15 Band around the waist (4)

DOWN

1 Vast, enormous (4)
2 Sprint, hurry, go fast (3)
4 Collection of maps in a book (5)
5 Make a picture of (4)
6 Courage (7)
9 Horrible (5)
10 Sheeplike horned animal (4)
11 Clean and tidy in appearance (4)
13 Put into service (3)

73

Letter Play

Try to work it out so each of the three-letter words in the list fits into the grid. If you do it correctly, each row of the grid will have two six-letter words.

DON **BAL** **MOT**
HER **ATE** **TEN**

	HER	

74

Word Ladder

Fill in each step with a genuine word, changing one letter at a time as you climb down from the top word to the bottom one. We've clued the steps for each ladder, but not in the correct order.

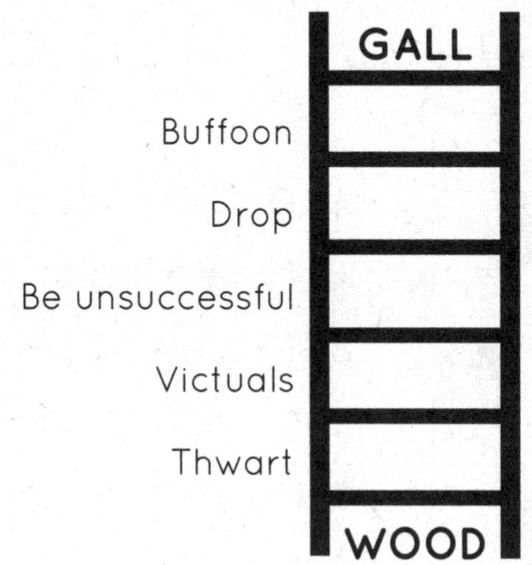

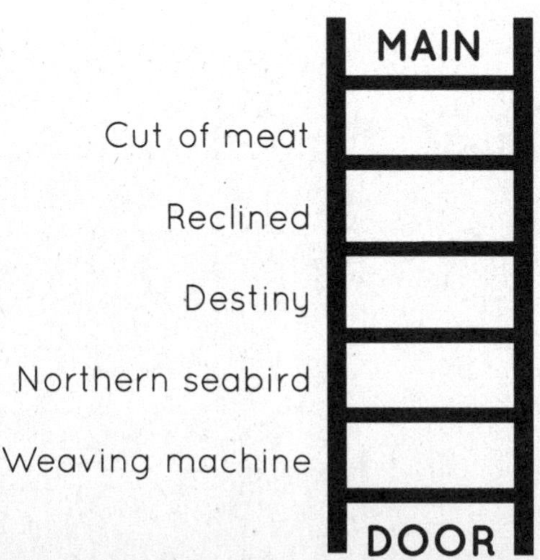

75

Fan-tas-tic

Solve the clues and enter your answers in the grid. Read down the letters in the shaded circles from top to bottom to find a new word.

Shaded clue: Something in the way

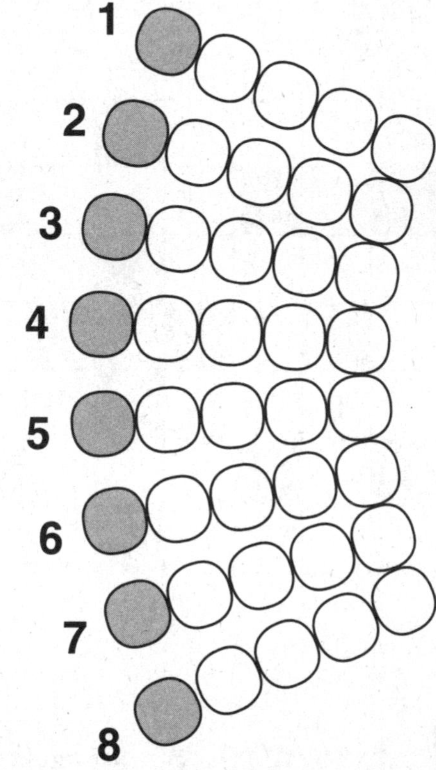

1 Barack ___, US president
2 Erect, construct
3 Long-bladed weapon
4 Robbery
5 Head of an abbey
6 Strategy board game
7 Yellow citrus fruit
8 Mistake

76

Slot 'n' Solve

Solve the clues and fit the answers into the grid, reading across. Then slot the printed three-letter words into the remaining spaces.

1 For eating off
2 Church walkway
3 Part of a flower
4 Vegetable that can make you cry
5 Stomach
6 Fish-eating mammal that has short, brown fur
7 Pop ____, band of musicians
8 Move to music

AGO AID ALL
ART BEG EEL
EGG ERN EYE
LOO NOT ODD
ONE POP RYE
SKI TON YAP

77

Slippery Anagrams

There are eight slippery words below, but the letters have all slid around. Can you unscramble them so that you are left with eight slippery items?

1 ANBNAA INSK
2 SEAREG
3 SHFI
4 CIE
5 ILO
6 SMSO
7 AOPS
8 DMU

78

1		2		3		4		
								5
6				7				
8					9	10		
				11				
12		13				14		
	15							

ACROSS

1 Strong wish for food (8)
6 Point placed over a letter of the alphabet (3)
7 Large musical instrument played by pressing narrow black or white bars (5)
8 Sound that bounces back (4)
9 Closed box used for cooking or baking (4)
12 Church singers (5)
14 Large body of salt water (3)
15 The bones of a human or animal forming the inner framework of the body (8)

DOWN

1 Spectators in a theater (8)
2 ____ black, totally dark (5)
3 Sort, kind (4)
4 Hot brown drink (3)
5 Artificial jet or stream of water that spouts from an opening (8)
10 Call on (5)
11 Spoken, not written (4)
13 Tree of the beech family that bears the acorn as its fruit (3)

79

Name Game

Complete the answers to these clues, then take the missing letters, in order, to spell out something edible.

1 Cinderella's prince	C _ _ R M I N G
2 Astonishment	A M A _ _ M E N T
3 Height	T A L _ _ E S S
4 Flute player	F L A _ _ I S T

80

Rhyme Time

The missing words in this rhyme are all to do with keeping warm and dry. Fill in the blanks using the rhyme to help you, then fit them in to the kriss kross grid in the usual way. The numbers in brackets show the number of letters in the missing words.

Some people wear a long over ______ (4), but it makes me feel good
When it's cold, to wear my anorak (6) with its nice fleecy ______ (4)
With a ______ (5) around my neck and wearing a warm ______ (7),
And a woolly ______ (3) on my head, I feel even better.
If the wind is chilly, I find my coldest bits
Are my fingers, so I like to wear warm ______ (6) or ______ (5).
My twin toddler brothers wear all-in-one padded ______ (5)
And if it's raining hard, we all wear Wellington ______ (5).
With thick ______ (5) inside them to keep our feet warm
We enjoy splashing through puddles and braving the storm.
But it feels good to reach home when it's pouring or sleeting
And find it's made cozy and warm by the central ______ (7).

A N O R A K

81

Change-a-Letter

Solve the clues below, in order, changing one letter of your answer each time to make a new word to fit the next clue. When you get around to clue 12, you will find that its answer is just one letter different from the first answer, DART.

1 ~~Small arrow~~
2 Homer Simpson's son
3 Tree-trunk covering
4 Public gardens
5 Fill a suitcase
6 Choose
7 Hit with the foot
8 ____ Jagger, famous singer
9 Small rodents
10 Game cubes
11 ____ Straits, pop group
12 Filth, grime

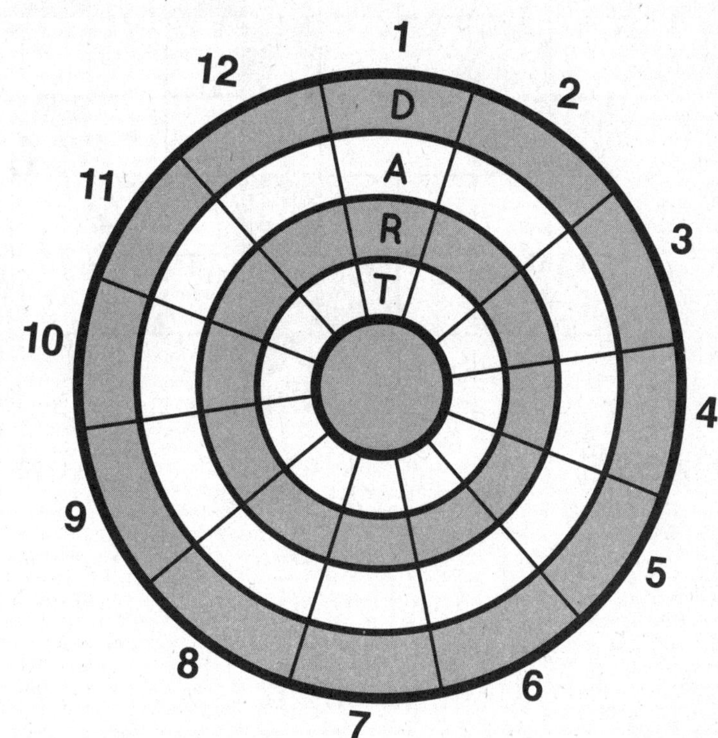

82

All Square

If you write the answers to these clues in the grid, you'll find that they read the same across and down.

1 Home or shelter of a wild animal
2 The organ of sight
3 An item for catching fish

1			
2			
3			

83

1		2		3		4	■	5	6		7
	■		■		■		■	■		■	
8			9		■		■	10			
	■	■		■	11					■	■
■	■	12					■		■	■	13
14				■		■	15		16		
	■		■	■		■		■		■	
17				■	18						

ACROSS

1 *Gulliver's* ____, book by Defoe (7)
5 Snatch (4)
8 Jeans material (5)
10 ____ game, not on home ground (4)
11 Tire slips (5)
12 Ships' floors (5)
14 Jumping insect (4)
15 Beam with pleasure (5)
17 Seldom seen (4)
18 Homes for dogs (7)

DOWN

1 Sea movement (4)
2 A girl's name (3)
3 Rough-leaved tall tree (3)
4 Shoes and ____, footwear (5)
6 Squabbles (4)
7 Spend money (3)
9 Brainwave (4)
10 ____ Levine, frontman of Maroon 5 (4)
11 Animal that makes a foul smell (5)
12 Animal like Bambi (4)
13 Hooks for hanging coats (4)
14 Distant (3)
15 Male child (3)
16 Skating surface (3)

84

Kriss Kross

Time to go to bed! Can you fit all the sleepy words in their correct places in the grid? If you fill in the eight-letter word, FATIGUED, that should help you to get started.

3 Letters
KIP
NAP

4 Letters
DOZY
ZIZZ

5 Letters
DREAM
TIRED

6 Letters
BUSHED
SLEEPY

7 Letters
DRAINED
LANGUID
SHUT-EYE
YAWNING

8 Letters
FATIGUED

9 Letters
EXHAUSTED
LETHARGIC
SHATTERED

85

Rhyming Rows

Work out the answers to the clues and write them in the spaces provided. In each row, the answers all rhyme. However, in each group of three, there is only one letter that appears in all three answers. If you write this letter in the box to the right of the grid, you will spell out a style of trousers.

1 Crossword question
2 Gnaw, munch
3 Dove's sound
4 Be in debt
5 Cut a lawn
6 Foot digit
7 Exercise room
8 Rather dark
9 __ Carrey, actor
~~10 Sphere~~
~~11 Smear~~
~~12 Soak up~~
13 Kayak
14 Cowboy's rope
15 Quarrel
16 Heaviness
17 __ Winslet, actress
18 Fish lure

1		2		3		
4		5		6		
7		8		9		
10	ORB	11	DAUB	12	ABSORB	B
13		14		15		
16		17		18		

86

Name Game

Complete the answers to these clues, then take the missing letters in order to spell out a type of insect.

1 Hedge or long grass cutters — S H _ _ R S
2 Country whose capital is Oslo — N O _ _ A Y
3 Clever — B R _ _ H T

87

Picture This

Write the name of each item pictured into the grid, then transfer the letters to the coded boxes in the lower grid. If you do this correctly, you will reveal a saying.

88

1		2		3		4	■	5	6		7
	■		■		■		■	■		■	
8			9		■		■	10			
	■	■		■	11					■	■
■	■	12					■		■	■	13
14				■		■	15		16		
	■		■	■		■		■		■	
17				■	18						

ACROSS

1 Horns of a deer (7)
5 Do as told (4)
8 Dark time of the day (5)
10 Cut with scissors (4)
11 ____ havoc, cause something bad to happen (5)
12 Black dots on sheets of music (5)
14 Item used in a stage play (4)
15 Barbed-wire ____, sharp barrier (4)
17 "He's ____ up and can't come home," he's busy (4)
18 Opposite of older (7)

DOWN

1 ___ Hathaway, actress (4)
2 Pull sharply (3)
3 Have food (3)
4 Wound marks on the skin (5)
6 Building where money is kept (4)
7 Puppy's cry (3)
9 Metal, wooden, or plastic ring (4)
10 Stop a goal from being scored (4)
11 Character in *Peter Pan* (5)
12 Nostrils' casing (4)
13 Time taken to orbit the sun (4)
14 Cooking container (3)
15 Nasty viral cold (3)
16 Keep complaining (3)

89

Ladderword

Work out the answers to the clues and write them in the grid. When you've finished, the letters in the gray column will spell an item of stationery you could use to draw.

1 A deep, round container with a flat bottom, an open top, and a handle
2 Ornament worn on the head by a king
3 Division of the stem of a tree
4 Organs of sight
5 Coverings for the hands
6 Animal related to the horse, but smaller and with longer ears

1						
	2					
3						
	4					
5						
6						

90

Add-a-Letter

Add a letter to each of the words so that they fit the clue. The six added letters will spell out a dance.

MINER		Gadget for chopping food
DEN		Head of a college
BAKER		Person in charge of money
LEAN		Free from dirt
WARD		Prize
PRICE		Royal male

91

Jigsaw

Can you fit the jigsaw pieces correctly in the grid so that there are six photography words reading across the rows? Here's a clue: One of the words is LENSES. The letters we've placed in the grid should help you get started.

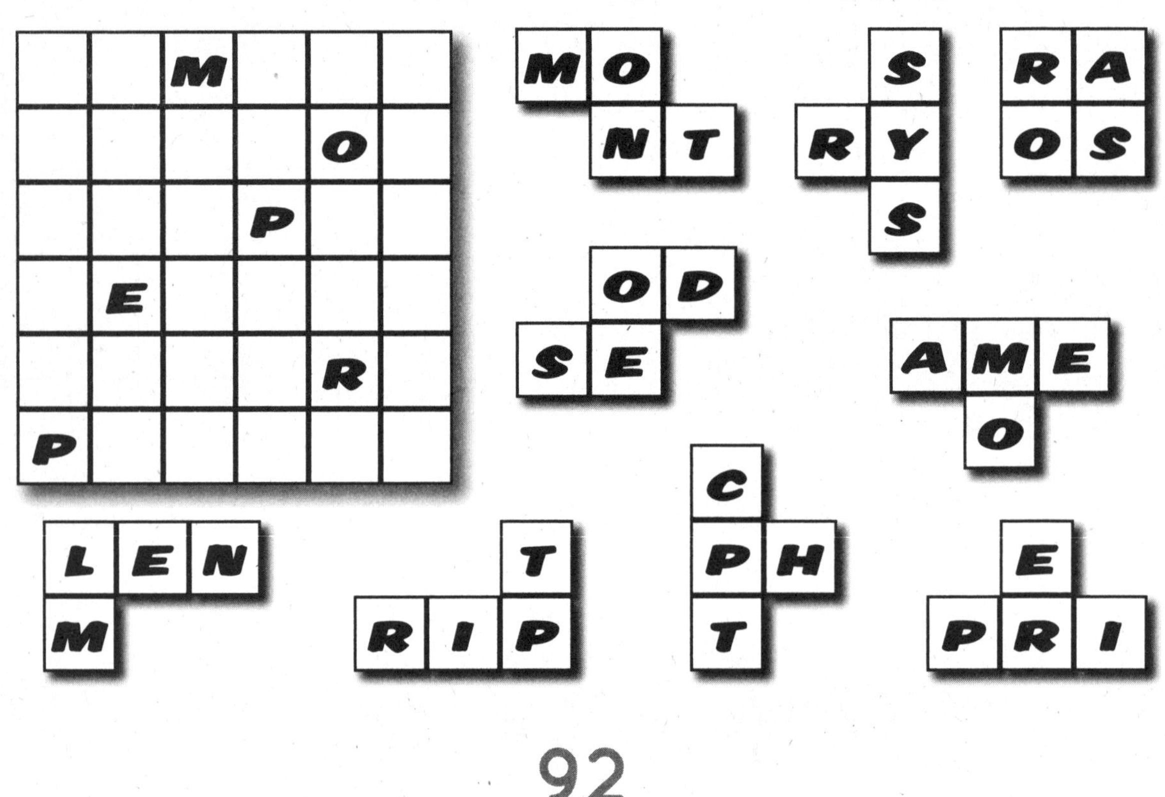

92

All Square

If you write the answers to these clues in the grid, you'll find that they read the same across and down.

1 Incapable of speech
2 A person who employs something
3 A drop of salty water produced by the eye
4 Makes a mistake

1				
2				
3				
4				

93

Code Cracker

In this puzzle, you must decide which letter of the alphabet is represented by each of the numbers from 1 to 26. We have already filled in two words, so you can see that T = 18, E = 19, A = 4, and so on. Begin by repeating these letters in each box where their numbers appear in the diagram. You will then have lots of letters to help you start guessing at likely words in the grid. All the letters of the alphabet will be used, so as you decide what each one is, cross it off at the side of the grid and enter it into the reference grid at the bottom. The completed grid will look like a filled-in crossword.

A	13	9	23	11	18		15		1	4	18	3	11	**N**
B	26		6		10	24	9	18	19		10		4	**O**
C	19	26	26	6	26		24		26	10	21	19	26	**P**
D	4		23		24	10	16	23	19		9		5	**Q**
E	14	24 N	19	19	2		6		18	4	25	19	2	**R**
F		10 U		20		6	15	21		5		22		**S**
G	3 C	26 R	4 A	18 T	19 E	26 R		4	1	4	18	19	16	**T**
H		2 S		26		1	6	8		12		3		**U**
I	3	19 E	16	4	26		25		7	19	2	18	2	**V**
J	26		26		4	15	4	26	19		9		15	**W**
K	6	3	19	4	24		17		26	4	16	9	6	**X**
L	15		4		3	26	10	5	1		21		26	**Y**
M	24	8	5	25	11		19		2	25	19	24	16	**Z**

1	2	3	4	5	6	7	8	9	10	11	12	13
	S	C	A						U			
14	**15**	**16**	**17**	**18**	**19**	**20**	**21**	**22**	**23**	**24**	**25**	**26**
				T	E					N		R

94

Ladderword

Write the answers to these clues, which are all to do with nature, in the grid, reading across. If you do this correctly, the letters in the shadowed column will spell out a type of fruit.

1 Big spotted cat
2 Jumping amphibian
3 Largest mammal that lives in the sea
4 Black-and-white treasure-collecting bird
5 "Laughing" animal
6 Evergreen tree
7 Bird that copies what you say
8 Swimming tortoise
9 Big cat with stripes
10 Baby cat

1
2
3
4
5
6
7
8
9
10

95

Word Ladder

Can you climb down the word ladder from BAD to LEG? Simply change one letter in BAD for the answer to the first clue, then one letter in that answer for the answer to the second clue, and so on.

CLUES

1 Furniture on which one sleeps
2 To ask, implore

	B	A	D
1			
2			
	L	E	G

96

Arroword

Write the answers to the clues starting in the squares shown by the arrows.

Automa-tic machine		Device to catch fish		A tool for digging		Wooden board	
				Edge, border		Unwell	
Flower and also a color		Rail transport					
			Lazy				
A container case		Nose's sense					

97

1		2	■	3		4
	■	5			■	
6			■	7		
	■	8			■	
9			■	10		

ACROSS

1 It joins foot to body (3)
3 Chewy candy (3)
5 Gases covering the earth (3)
6 Male sheep (3)
7 World's second-largest bird (3)
8 Lamb's mother (3)
9 Word of agreement (3)
10 Equipment (3)

DOWN

1 Truck (5)
2 Olympic ____, international event (5)
3 Language spoken in Greece (5)
4 ____ Everest, world's highest peak (5)

98

1		2		3	■	4		5
	■		■	6	7		■	
8			■	9				
	■	■	10	■		■	■	
11		12		13	■	14		
	■	15			■		■	
16			■	17				

ACROSS

1 Go to the ____, be first (5)
4 Part of the mouth (3)
6 Night before (3)
8 Pen fluid (3)
9 Enthusiastic (5)
11 Snapshot (5)
14 Everything (3)
15 Pigs' home (3)
16 Long-tailed rodent (3)
17 Opposite of late (5)

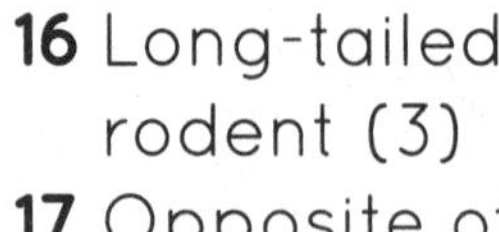

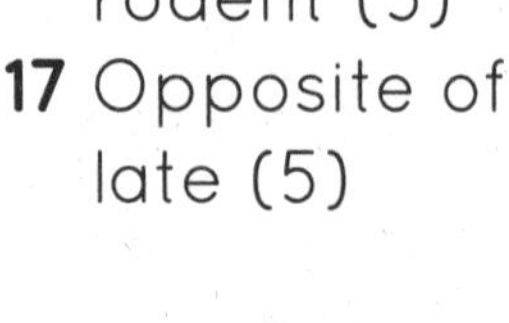

DOWN

1 Fin of a dolphin (7)
2 Shipbuilding timber (3)
3 Peg for a golf ball (3)
4 Lower limb (3)
5 Type of herb (7)
7 Small truck (3)
10 Had a meal (3)
12 Select as an alternative (3)
13 The first number (3)
14 On the ____, being broadcast (3)

99

Word Link

Starting at the top left, fit the names of the objects into the diagram so that the last letter of one word is the first letter of the next. But watch out, the pictures are not in order.

100

Double Trouble...

In this puzzle, two kriss kross grids have been mixed up. You have to decide which words fit in which grid, but two words have been entered to give you a start. What a dilemma!

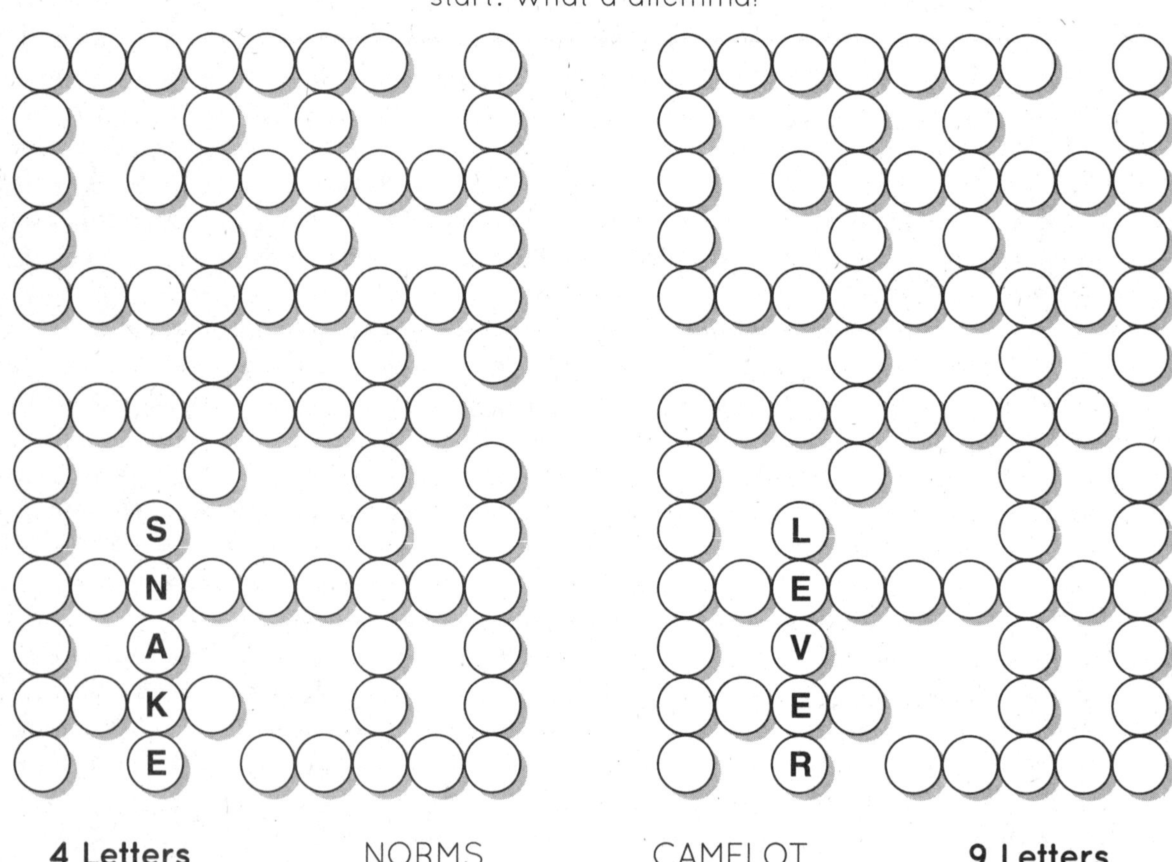

4 Letters
OMEN
TAKE

5 Letters
ABLER
ENDOW
GLORY
GRAFT
~~LEVER~~
LUNAR
NORMS
~~SNAKE~~

6 Letters
BISTER
CEDARS
FELLOW
PLEASE

7 Letters
ANIMATE
CAMELOT
EMERGED
GLIDING
GRADUAL
ISOLATE

8 Letters
ABSENTEE
CAMELLIA
DEMANDED
DESERTER

9 Letters
EYELASHES
MUNICIPAL
OVERSPEND
TEARDROPS
TRIATHLON
YOUNGSTER

101

Picture This

Write the name of each item pictured into the grid, then transfer the letters to the coded boxes in the lower grid. If you do this correctly, you will reveal a color.

102

X-word

The answers to these four clues are all five-letter words ending in **E**, the center letter. Write the answers in the grid, starting from the outer squares, then rearrange the letters in the shaded squares to spell out an item of clothing.

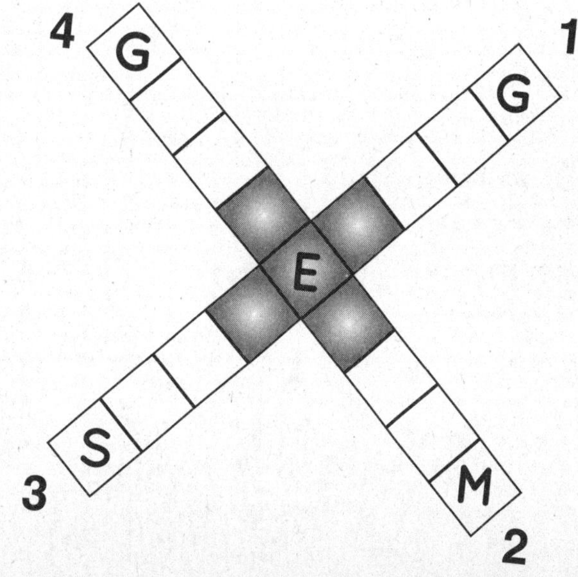

1 Bird found on a farm
2 Rodent
3 Result of a football game
4 Person who shows tourists around

103

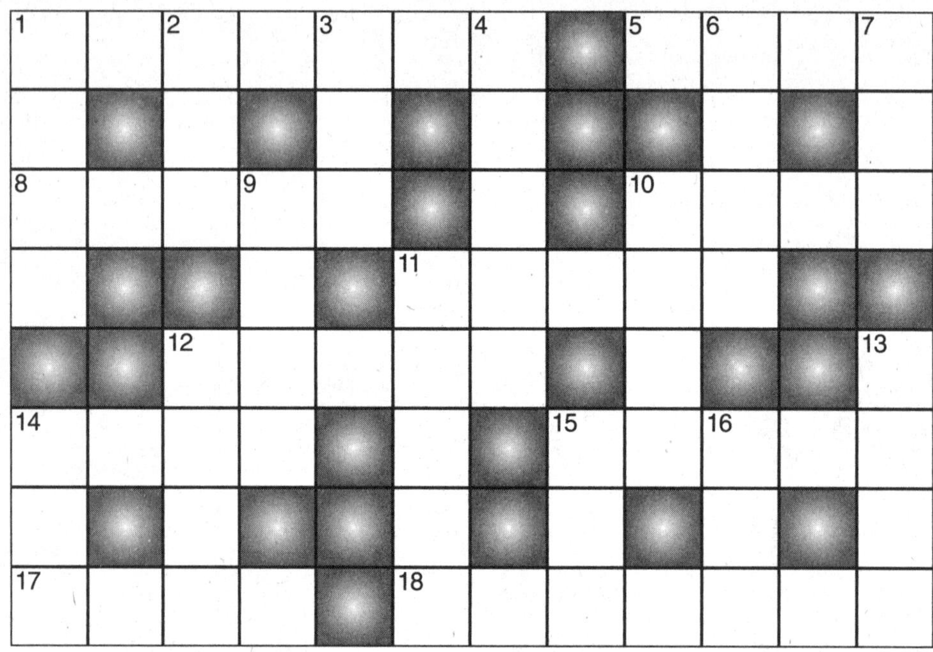

ACROSS

1 Crushing food between teeth (7)
5 On top of (4)
8 Part of a tree (5)
10 Food seasoning (4)
11 Quick meal (5)
12 Sugary cake decoration (5)
14 Fast-running animal (4)
15 Small, edible sea creature (5)
17 Permit (4)
18 Highest (building) (7)

DOWN

1 Important town (4)
2 Flightless Australian bird (3)
3 Writing liquid (3)
4 ____, ____, gone (auctioneer's call) (5)
6 Mountain top (4)
7 Hard-shelled fruit (3)
9 Pleasant, enjoyable (4)
10 Wound mark on the skin (4)
11 Animal's nose (5)
12 Colored part of the eye (4)
13 Use needles and wool (4)
14 Thigh joint (3)
15 Chum (3)
16 Top playing card (3)

104

ACROSS

6 Disappointing, annoying (11)
7 Not easily disturbed, calm (6)
8 Coal pit (4)
9 Junior officer (5)
11 Not clean (5)
13 Adjoin, border on (4)
15 Coming every year (6)
17 Period in which some animals spend the winter sleeping (11)

DOWN

1 Spoken examination (4)
2 Human soul, mind, or spirit (6)
3 Crossword diagram, or network (4)
4 Tiny particle (4)
5 Untangle (6)
10 Although (6)
12 Set light to (6)
14 Layer of a cake (4)
15 Parent's sister (4)
16 Run _____, be in a frenzy (4)

105

Word Ladder

Can you climb down the word ladder from CALL to TELL? Simply change one letter in CALL for the answer to the first clue, then one letter in that answer for the answer to the second clue, and so on.

CLUES

1 Entrance area in a house
2 Round toy
3 Opposite of short

106

Leftover Letters

The answers to the clues in the two grids contain all the same letters, except for one. Write the leftover letters in the end column to find out the name of a famous cartoon rabbit.

1 Begin • It twinkles
2 Spring month • Squeeze into
3 Yell at • Hit with bullet
4 School tests • Tools used to cut logs
5 Flower part • Story
6 Sugary • Compass point
7 Massive, big • Blustery wind

1	S	T	A	R	T
2					
3					
4					
5					
6					
7					

S	T	A	R

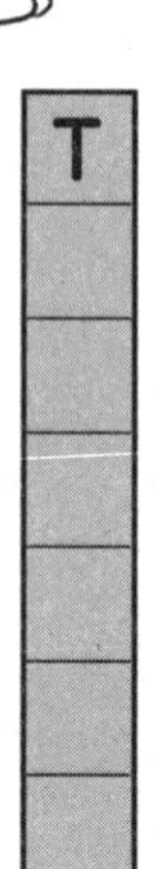

This sign (•) separates the clues for the first and second grids.

107

Name Game

Complete the answers to these clues, then take the missing letters in order to spell out the name of a mountain.

1 Red salad fruit	T O _ _ T O
2 Crispy coating on cooked fish	B A _ _ E R
3 Sound system	S T _ _ E O
4 Teacher's workplace	S C _ _ O L
5 Big wasp	H O _ _ E T

108

Code Cracker

In this puzzle, you must decide which letter of the alphabet is represented by each of the numbers from 1 to 26. We have already filled in one word, so you can see that E = 9, Q = 7, U = 15, and so on. Begin by repeating these letters in each box where their numbers appear in the diagram. You will then have lots of letters to help you start guessing at likely words in the grid. All the letters of the alphabet will be used, so as you decide what each one is, cross it off at the side of the grid and enter it into the reference grid at the bottom. The completed grid will look like a filled-in crossword.

A	16	12	24	2	6	13		5	19	18	9	17	20	N
B	12		1		5		1		15		3		9	O
C	9	18	9		25	3	5	6	4		4	24	19	P
D	9				9		8		9				24	Q
E	23	9	10	11			3			2	9 E	17	15	R
F	9		24			6	9	14			7 Q		2	S
G		5	19	11	21	20		5	16	25	15 U	3		T
H	11		14			13	5	21			5 A		9	U
I	25	3	9	26			6			6	3 L	5	2	V
J	25				22		24		8				9	W
K	1	15	8		11	3	19	9	10		9	5	10	X
L	15		13		3		9		5		2		14	Y
M	20	16	9	17	20	13		5	19	22	15	10	9	Z

1	2	3	4	5	6	7	8	9	10	11	12	13
		L		A		Q		E				
14	**15**	**16**	**17**	**18**	**19**	**20**	**21**	**22**	**23**	**24**	**25**	**26**
	U											

109

Word Ladder

Fill in each step with a genuine word, changing one letter at a time as you climb down from the top word to the bottom one. We've clued the steps for each ladder, but not in the correct order.

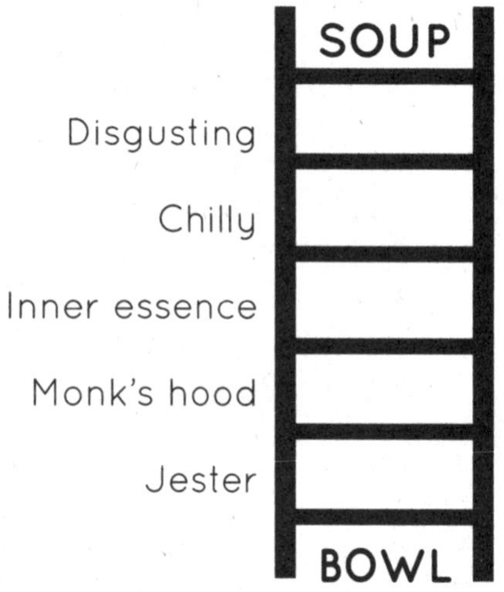

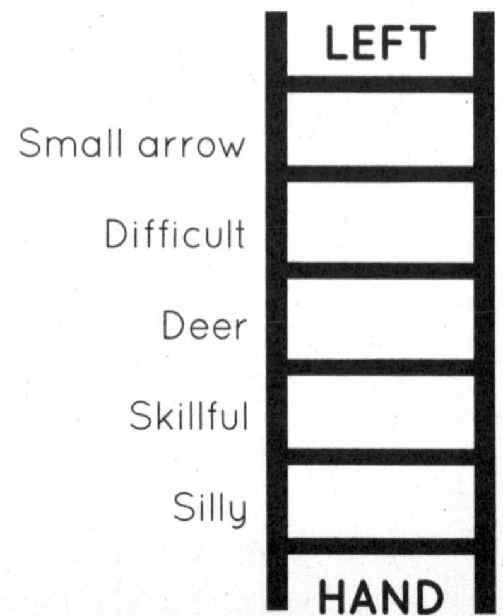

110

Fan-tas-tic

Solve the clues and enter your answers in the grid. Read the letters in the shaded circles from top to bottom to find a new word.
Shaded clue: Bounce around

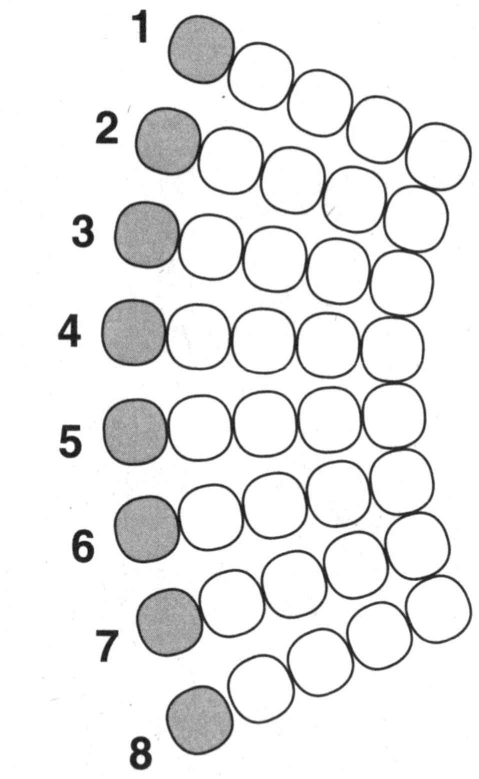

1 Crowlike bird
2 House of ice
3 King's headgear
4 Poppy drug
5 Scrap of bread
6 Residence
7 Vacant
8 Popular dinner fish

111

Picture Puzzle

Write the name of each item pictured into the grid, and the circled letters will spell out a traditional British Christmas dessert.

112

Spiral Puzzle

Fit the answers into the grid—the last letter of one answer is the first of the next.

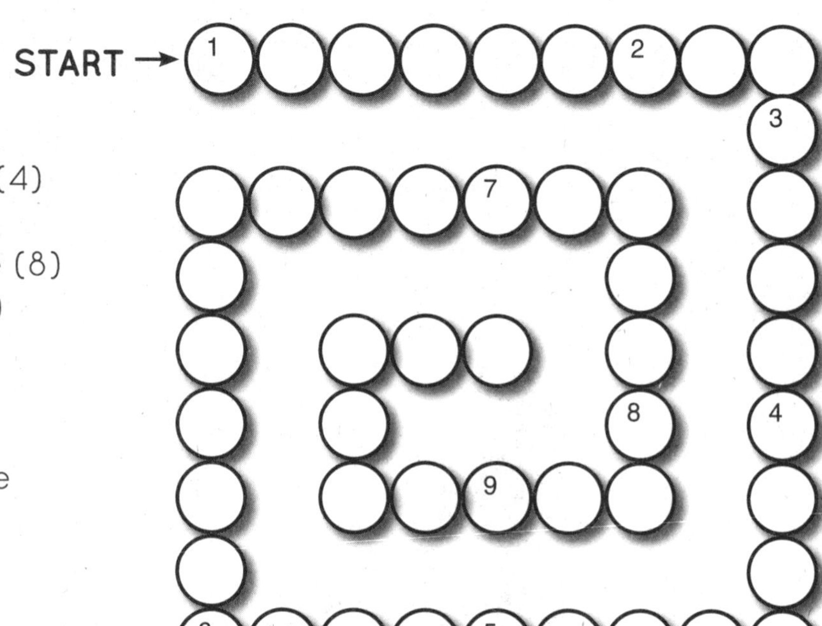

1 Green jewel (7)
2 Daybreak, sunrise (4)
3 After dark (5)
4 Three-sided shape (8)
5 Bird with talons (5)
6 School test (11)
7 Almost (6)
8 Twelve months (4)
9 Colorful arch in the sky (7)

113

ACROSS

2 Monarch (4)
4 Short skirt (4)
5 To transfer to another's custody or charge (7)
6 Louse eggs (4)
7 To hit hard, as in boxing (4)

DOWN

1 Key, important (7)
2 Caressing (7)
3 Pieces (of gold) (7)

114

It's a Fact!

The answers to these clues must be written across the rows of boxes in the grid. As you fill in the grid, transfer your letters to the coded boxes in the lower grid. If you do this correctly, you will reveal an interesting fact.

1 First ____, emergency treatment
2 Mom or Dad's sister
3 ____ constrictor, snake
4 Ten minus two
5 Animal's coat
6 Type of short coat
7 Morning, in short
8 Not any
9 Small horse

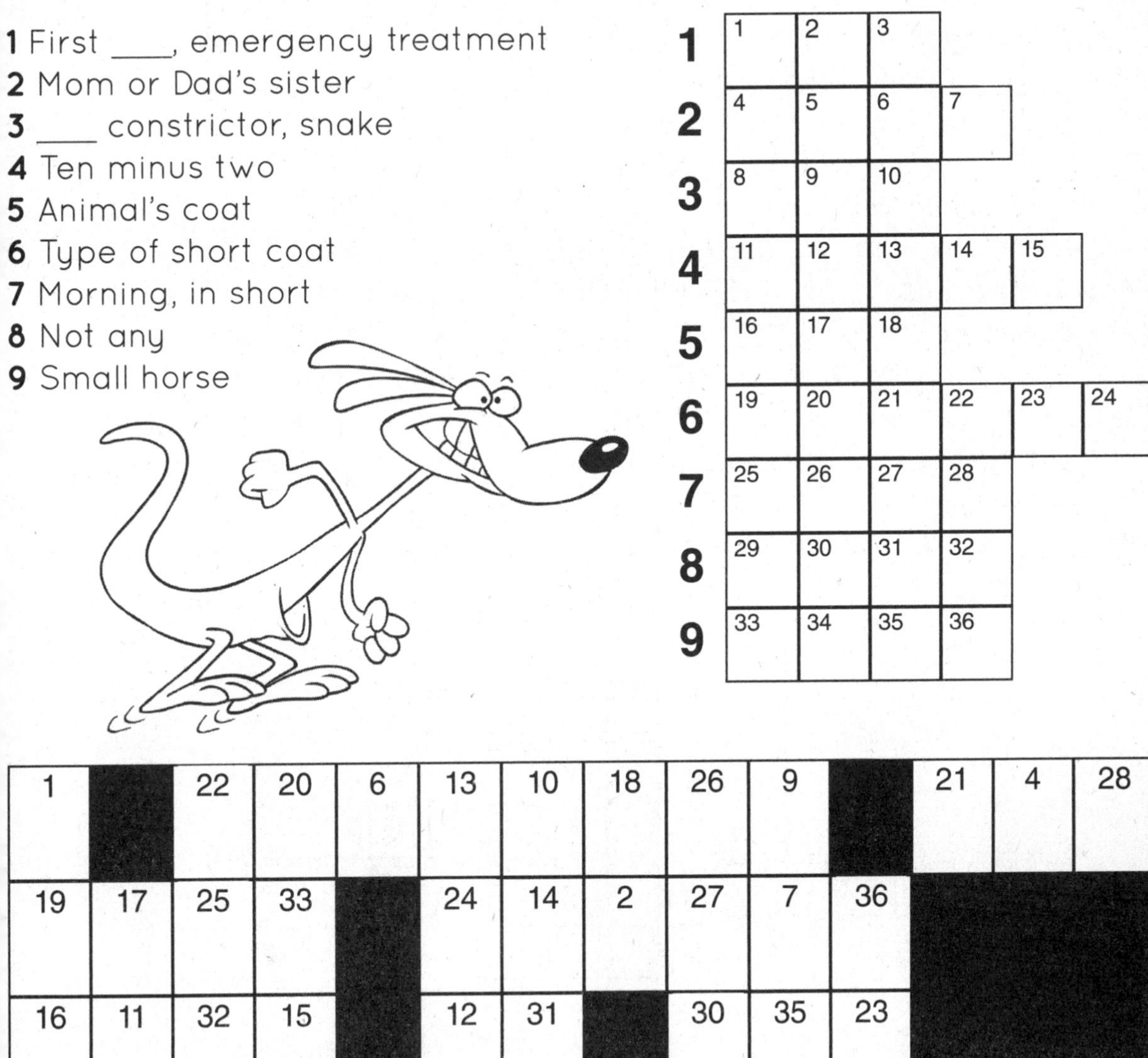

1	1	2	3			
2	4	5	6	7		
3	8	9	10			
4	11	12	13	14	15	
5	16	17	18			
6	19	20	21	22	23	24
7	25	26	27	28		
8	29	30	31	32		
9	33	34	35	36		

1	■	22	20	6	13	10	18	26	9	■	21	4	28
19	17	25	33	■	24	14	2	27	7	36	■	■	■
16	11	32	15	■	12	31	■	30	35	23	■	■	■
8	34	5	29	3									

115

Rhyme Time

The missing words in this rhyme are all connected with having a meal out. Fill them in, using the rhyme to help you, and then fit them in the kriss kross grid in the usual way. The numbers in brackets show the number of letters in the missing words.

Last Saturday in town, Mom said, at one o'clock we'll all meet
For lunch (5), at the self-service ______ (10) where we usually ______ (3)
The ______ (4) was printed on a board, with each item's ____ (5)
So we worked out what our meals would cost,
then chose something nice.
We each took what we wanted and slid it along on a ______ (4)
And added a fizzy ______ (5), then Mom went up to the till to ____ (3).
We picked up knives, ______ (5), spoons, and straws, and then we found
A ______ (5) at the window we could all fit around.
We all enjoyed our meals—at that café, they're always good,
But sometimes we go to another that has tasty ______ (4).
It's not self-service, instead a ______ (6) serves you, and he will
Bring your order to you, and at the end he brings the ______ (4).

L U N C H

116

Word Link

Starting at the top left, fit the names of the objects into the diagram so that the last letter of one word is the first letter of the next. But watch out, the pictures are not in order.

117

Kriss Kross

See how quickly you can fit all these words relating to star signs into the grid.

3 Letters
LEO
RAM

4 Letters
FISH
LION

5 Letters
ARIES
LIBRA
VIRGO

6 Letters
CANCER
GEMINI
MAIDEN
PISCES
SCALES
TAURUS
ZODIAC

7 Letters
SCORPIO

8 Letters
AQUARIUS
SCORPION

9 Letters
CAPRICORN

11 Letters
SAGITTARIUS

118

ACROSS

3 Steals (7)
5 Whichever one (3)
6 White lie (3)
8 Branch out (6)

DOWN

1 Silly people (7)
2 Sent ____, dismissed (3)
4 Prevails (6)
7 Health resort (3)

119

ACROSS

6 Hotel cleaning lady (11)
7 Cold symptom (6)
8 Large brass instrument (4)
9 Sugary (5)
11 Loiter (5)
13 Summons (4)
15 Greatly (6)
17 One before the last (11)

DOWN

1 Part of face below the mouth (4)
2 Obstruct (6)
3 Yield (4)
4 Fail to include (4)
5 Wood (6)
10 Prison guard (6)
12 Suppose without knowing (6)
14 Not false (4)
15 Right to reject (4)
16 Not on time (4)

120

All Square

If you write the answers to these clues in the grid, you'll find that they read the same across and down.

1 Group of people forming a side in a game
2 In addition to persons or things mentioned
3 Requests information
4 A dirty or untidy mass

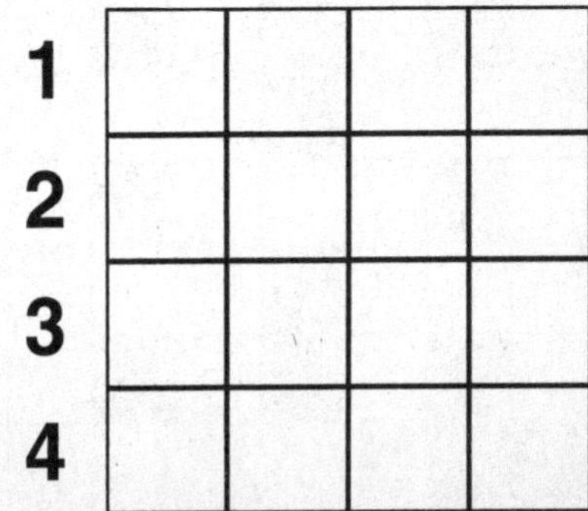

121

ACROSS

6 Survey (6)
7 Sloping access (4)
8 Solid square-faced object (4)
9 Time leading up to Christmas (6)
10 Putting one's own interests first (11)
13 Seal off (6)
15 Rear deck of a ship (4)
16 Pipe (4)
17 Castle tower (6)

DOWN

1 Safe (6)
2 Area of land isolated in water (4)
3 Kill a person for political reasons (11)
4 Tried and tested (6)
5 Word ending a prayer (4)
11 Animal food (6)
12 Tool like a spade (6)
14 Responsibility (4)
15 Town possessing a harbor (4)

122

ACROSS

1 Bound with sticky ribbon (5)
5 Major armed conflict (3)
6 Mouth edge (3)
7 The whole (3)
8 Nick (3)
9 Veneration (3)
10 Provide with (5)

DOWN

1 Hauling (6)
2 Biblical story (7)
3 Slow-witted person (7)
4 Per item (6)

123

Picture This

Write the name of each item pictured into the grid, and the circled letters will spell out the favorite plant of this friendly Scottish bagpiper.

124

Rhyming Rows

Work out the answers to the clues and write them in the spaces provided. In each row, the answers all rhyme. However, in each group of three, there is only one letter that appears in all three answers. If you write this letter in the box to the right of the grid, you'll find something that can be very beautiful. One group of three has been filled in to start you off.

1 Paper handkerchief	**2** Footwear	**3** Cowboy's rope
4 Not me	**5** Strong sticky adhesive	**6** Not false
~~**7** Cat family animal~~	~~**8** Egyptian statue~~	~~**9** Skating arenas~~
10 Changes color	**11** Men, boys, fellows	**12** Fibs
13 Turn to ice	**14** Grab	**15** Small green veggies
16 Friend, pal	**17** Used to attract fish	**18** Two times four

1		2		3		
4		5		6		
7	LYNX	8	SPHINX	9	RINKS	N
10		11		12		
13		14		15		
16		17		18		

125

Name Game

Complete the answers to these clues, then take the missing letters in order to spell out the name of a state.

1 Truthful or sincere	H O _ _ S T
2 Opponents, competitors	R I _ _ L S
3 Item awarded as a sign of victory	M E _ _ L S

126

ACROSS

1 Hot chocolate (5)
4 Point at a target (3)
6 Male child (3)
8 Animal's foot (3)
9 Toys flown in the wind (5)
11 Traffic's "caution" color (5)
14 Ewe's cry (3)
15 Single number (3)
16 This very minute (3)
17 Piece of snow (5)

DOWN

1 Master of a ship (7)
2 Calf's mother (3)
3 Inquire (3)
4 Common insect (3)
5 Error (7)
7 Frying liquid (3)
10 Egg-laying fowl (3)
12 Arrow-firing weapon (3)
13 Umpire (3)
14 ____ constrictor, snake (3)

127

Picture Crossword

Have a look at the objects in the left-hand grid and decide what they are. Then take the first letter of each object and put it in the corresponding place in the grid on the right. The completed grid should look like a filled-in crossword.

128

Quest

All the answers to the clues are four-letter words and you have to enter them into the grid, starting from the outer squares. When you have done that, you will find some fruit reading clockwise around the innermost squares from number 9.

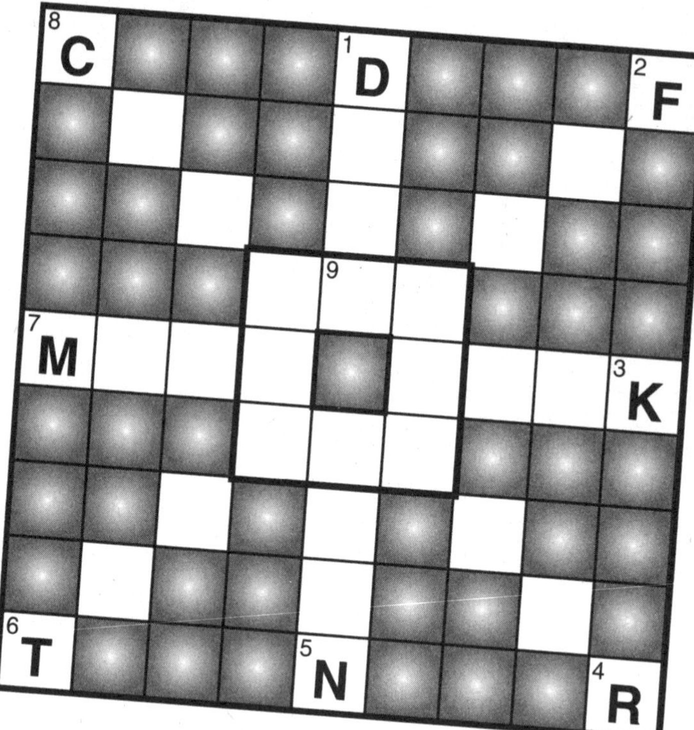

1 Compact ___, music equipment
2 Cod or haddock, for example
3 ____ Winslet, *Titanic* actress
4 Lion's noise
5 Close by
6 Cab, hire car
7 Pal, friend
8 Felines

129

Take Five

The answers to these clues are all five-letter words. Enter them into the grid, reading across, and the letters in the diagonal row of shaded boxes should spell out something edible.

1 Longest bone in the human body
2 Bow and _____
3 ____ Mars, singer
4 Spring month
5 Phantom, spook

1					
2					
3					
4					
5					

130

ACROSS

6 Four-armed Hindu deity (6)
7 Part to play (4)
8 Terrible (4)
9 Drink popular at Christmas (6)
10 Diploma (11)
13 Cloth (6)
15 Welsh national vegetable (4)
16 Extinct bird (4)
17 Shrewd (6)

DOWN

1 Figure of speech, comparing one thing to another (6)
2 Item of footwear (4)
3 Lacking sincerity (11)
4 Extremely sad (6)
5 In addition (4)
11 Great fear (6)
12 Formal agreement (6)
14 Before long (4)
15 Tardy (4)

131

All Square

If you write the answers to these clues in the grid, you'll find that they read the same across and down.

1 Nothing, not any
2 The opposite of odd
3 True, genuine, authentic
4 Without others or anything further; exclusively

1				
2				
3				
4				

132

ACROSS

1 Dog's foot, for example (3)
2 Domestic animal (3)
5 Huge, gigantic (7)
6 Extremely old (7)
8 Jump on one leg (3)
9 Amusement, entertaining (3)

DOWN

1 Tree on which dates are found (4)
3 Honest, sincere (4)
4 Pillow for a sofa (7)
6 Curved part of a gateway (4)
7 Area that is larger than a village and smaller than a city (4)

1				2		3
			4			
5						
6						7
8				9		

133

Letter Play

Try to work out where each of the three-letter words in the list fits into the grid. If you do it correctly, each line of the grid will have two six-letter words.

MAN **GER** **GAR**
AGE **NER** **NDA**

	MAN	

134

Word Link

Starting at the top left, fit the names of the objects into the diagram so that the last letter of one word is the first letter of the next. But watch out, the pictures are not in order.

135

Arroword

Write the answers to the clues starting in the squares shown by the arrows.

Funny magazine		Work, occupation		Woody perennial plant	Rescue from danger	Gas and oil, e.g.	
						Child or young goat	
Android machines		Vehicle's stopping device					
			Cruel and mean				
Container for rubbish		Unwanted plants					

136

Blazing Anagrams

There are eight words related to fire below, but the letters have all been mixed up. Can you unscramble them?

1 MALFE
2 FACEPERIL
3 SESHA
4 RINNBUG
5 GLIBANZ
6 TAHERE
7 BIFENOR
8 KOSME

137

Write the answers to the clues in the grid. Then rearrange the letters in the shaded squares for the name of a famous dog.

ACROSS

1 Something strange or not known (7)
4 Venetian ____, type of window covering (5)
5 Section of a book (7)
8 Three-legged chair (5)
9 Imaginary bird that sets fire to itself and is born again (7)

DOWN

1 Sorcery (5)
2 Communication device invented by Alexander Graham Bell (9)
3 Wash in clear water (5)
6 Rabbit cage (5)
7 Unwind, take it easy (5)

1	●		2		3	
	■	■		■		■
	■	4			●	
	■	■		■		■
5	6		●			7
■		■		■	■	
8 ●		●			■	
■		■		■	■	
9		●				

The famous dog is: _ _ _ _ _ _ _ _ _ !

138

Word Ladder

Can you climb down the ladder from COLD to HEAT? Just change one letter in COLD for the answer to the first clue, then one letter in that answer for the answer to the second clue, and so on.

CLUES

1 Young horse
2 Winter garment
3 River around a castle
4 Animal flesh

	C	O	L	D
1				
2				
3				
4				
	H	E	A	T

139

ACROSS

1 Smell, perfume (5)
4 Postage token (5)
7 Short sleep (3)
8 Large area of salt water (3)
9 Illustration in an atlas (3)
10 Small burrowing creature (4)
11 Book or film's name (5)
14 Watchful, wide awake (5)
16 Profound (4)
18 Equipment, outfit (3)
20 Earth's atmosphere (3)
21 Pull (a vehicle) (3)
22 Move rhythmically to music (5)
23 Girl's garment (5)

DOWN

1 Yellow grains on a beach (4)
2 Investigate new territory (7)
3 Sense in the mouth (5)
4 Opposite of finish (5)
5 Goal, ambition, target (3)
6 Salt and ____, seasonings (6)
12 Supporting tower of a bridge (7)
13 Made a noise like a dog (6)
15 Make fun of (5)
16 Had the courage (5)
17 Nocturnal birds reputed to be wise (4)
19 Darkening of the skin in sunlight (3)

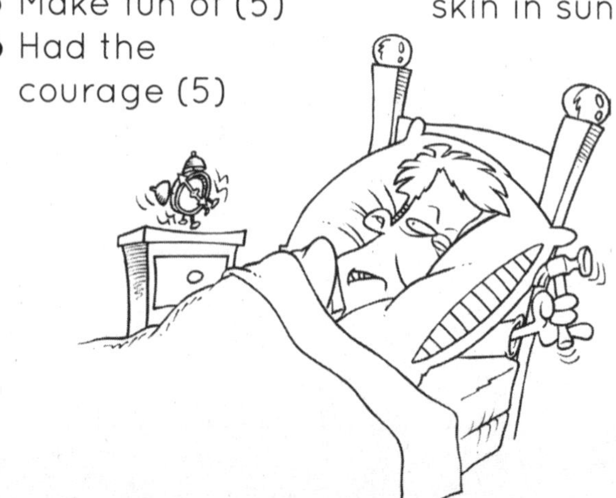

140

Just the Job

Follow the letter trails from each of these people to find out what they do for a living.

141

Kriss Kross

Solve the kriss kross by filling in all the words related to bread. Start with the 12-letter word, PUMPERNICKEL. When you've finished, write down the letters in the green squares to spell another type of bread that is served in just about every meal in the Middle East.

3 Letters
BAP
BUN
COB

4 Letters
NAAN

5 Letters
BAGEL
SCONE

7 Letters
BLOOMER
TEACAKE

8 Letters
BAGUETTE
CIABATTA
FOCACCIA
TORTILLA

9 Letters
CROISSANT
PANETTONE

12 Letters
PUMPERNICKEL

The other type of bread is: _ _ _ _ !

142

Picture This

Write the name of each item pictured into the grid. Once you've done that, the circled letters can be rearranged to spell out what kind of weather is forecast.

143

ACROSS

1 Lump of firewood (3)
3 Strong, healthy (3)
5 Odd or weird (7)
6 Gold ____, award for first place (5)
9 Object that you put to your lips and blow (7)
10 Large cup used for drinking tea (3)
11 Skin injury (3)

DOWN

1 After all others (4)
2 Hobby for green-fingered people (9)
3 ____ *Four,* superhero film (9)
4 At that time (4)
7 Move through water (like fish) (4)
8 Have a break (4)

144

Word Ladder

Can you climb down the word ladder from WET to DRY? Simply change one letter in WET for the answer to the first clue, then one letter in that answer for the answer to the second clue, and so on.

CLUES

1 To make a wager, gamble
2 Flying nocturnal mammal
3 Body of water enclosed by a curve of the coast around it
4 Opposite of night

	W	E	T
1			
2			
3			
4			
	D	R	Y

145

Spooky Puzzle

Complete the words in the two grids and the white squares will reveal the name of a famous ghost.

	A	M	M	E	R
	A	S	I	N	G
	T	T	A	C	K
	R	A	G	O	N
	I	Z	A	R	D
	F	F	O	R	T
	T	R	I	N	G
	U	N	D	A	Y

	I	C	C	U	P
	X	Y	G	E	N
	E	C	O	R	D
	H	I	V	E	R
	S	C	A	P	E
	A	G	P	I	E
	C	T	I	O	N
	E	E	D	L	E

146

ACROSS

2 Secret writing (4)
4 Shrub (4)
5 Curved gateway (4)
6 Order of knights in *Star Wars* (4)
7 Nibbles, bites (4)
8 Catch, tear (4)

DOWN

1 Operating doctor (7)
2 Pursuing (7)
3 Leaves suddenly and often secretly (7)

147

Jigsaw

Can you fit the jigsaw pieces in the grid correctly so that there are six words connected to cats reading across the rows? Here's a clue: One of the words is SPHYNX. The letters we've placed in the grid should help you get started.

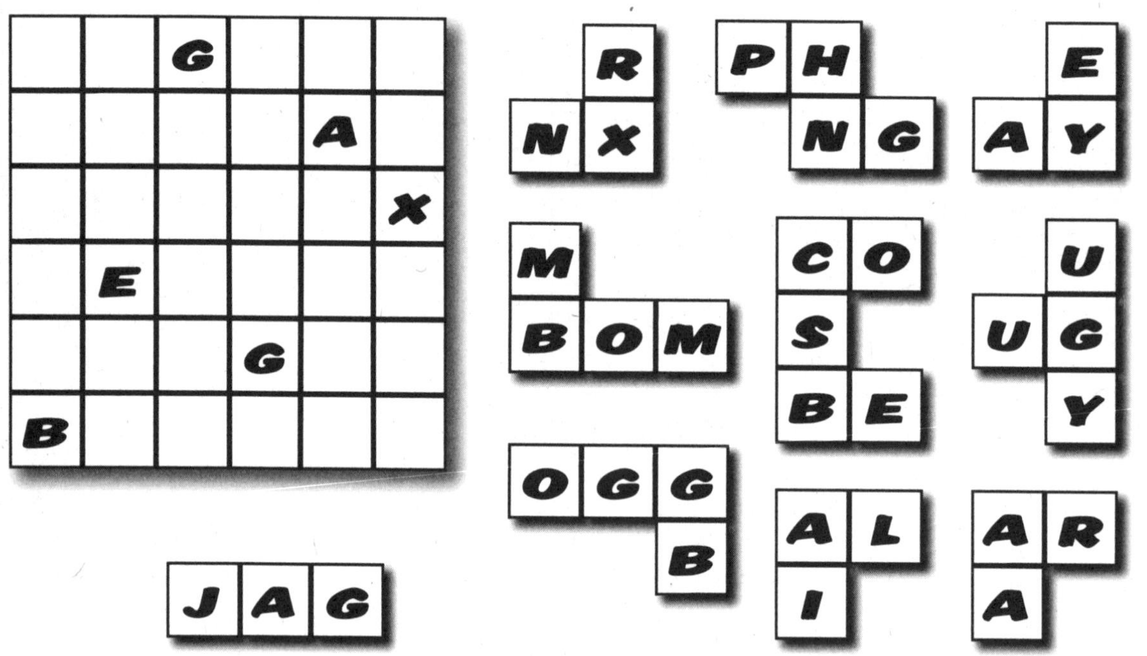

148

ACROSS

4 Get to your destination (6)
5 Rocket-launching weapon (7)
8 Witches' laugh (6)

DOWN

1 A young sheep (4)
2 Separate from your spouse (7)
3 Seven days (4)
6 A curved construction over an opening (4)
7 Word that ends a prayer (4)

149

Word Link

Starting at the top left, fit the names of the objects into the diagram so that the last letter of one word is the first letter of the next. But watch out, the pictures are not in order.

150

Arroword

Write the answers to the clues starting in the squares shown by the arrows.

Long, scaly reptile	↓	Small branches	↓	Water in a solid state	Items around the neck	Cash	↓
Enchanter, wizard		Clever humor →		↓	↓	Make inquiries	
↳						↓	
Honey-making insect		Large farm birds →					
↳				Upper atmosphere →			

151

Take Five

The answers to these clues are all five-letter words. Enter them into the grid, reading across, and the letters in the diagonal row of shaded boxes should spell out a word related to plants.

1 Stairs
2 Thin piece of wood
3 Fruit that wine is made from
4 Little
5 Trail

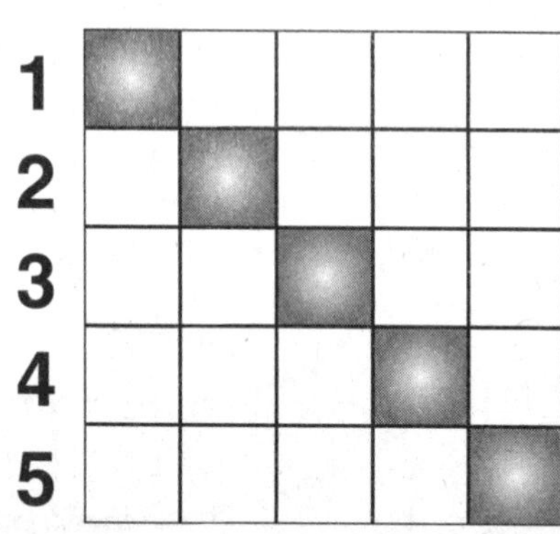

152

Kriss Kross

See how quickly you can fit all the composers listed below into the interlocking grid. We've given you a starter word to help you out.

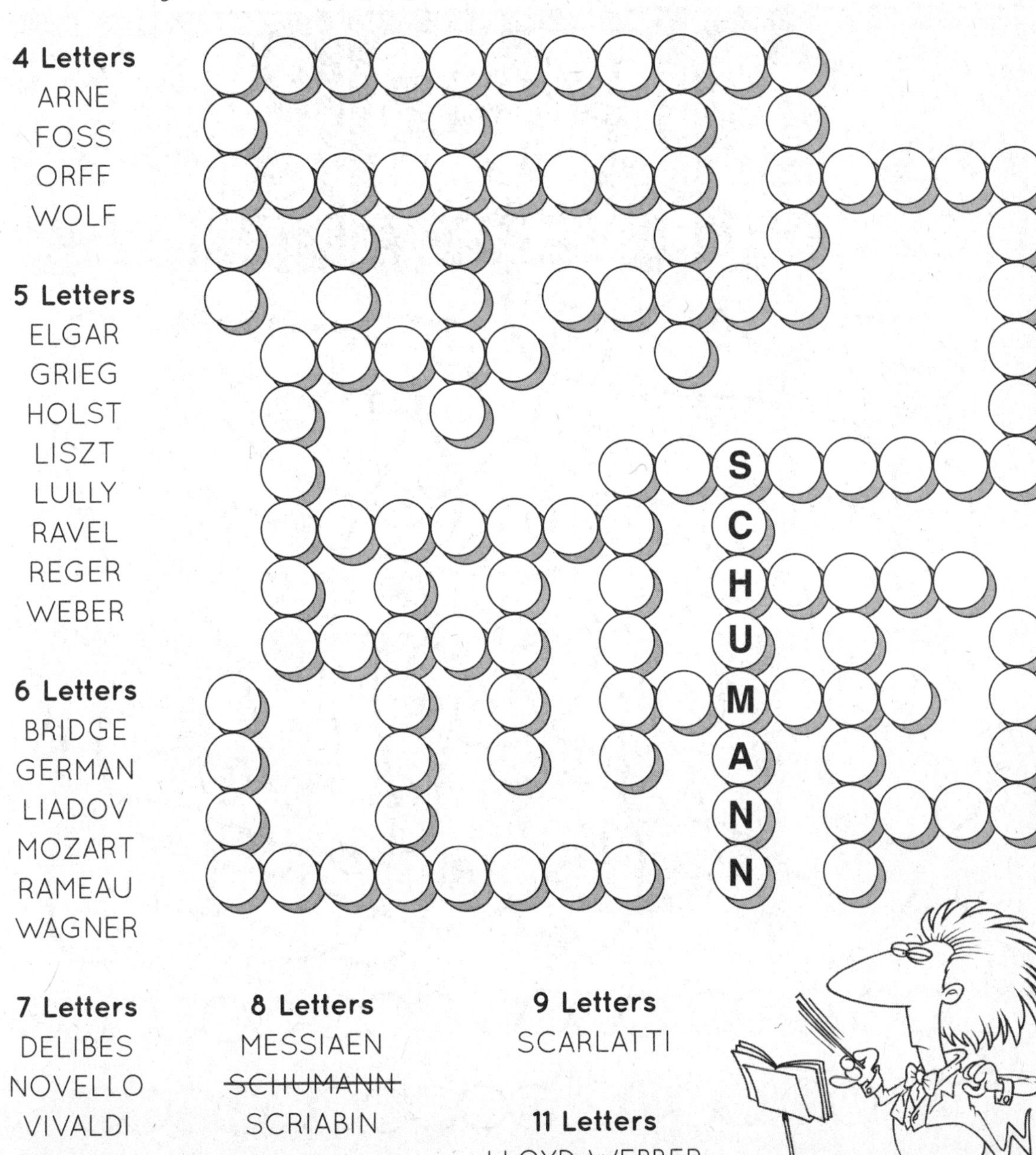

4 Letters
ARNE
FOSS
ORFF
WOLF

5 Letters
ELGAR
GRIEG
HOLST
LISZT
LULLY
RAVEL
REGER
WEBER

6 Letters
BRIDGE
GERMAN
LIADOV
MOZART
RAMEAU
WAGNER

7 Letters
DELIBES
NOVELLO
VIVALDI

8 Letters
MESSIAEN
~~SCHUMANN~~
SCRIABIN

9 Letters
SCARLATTI

11 Letters
LLOYD WEBBER

153

Commercial Break

Follow the trails to find out what each of these TV ads has to say about its fantastic product.

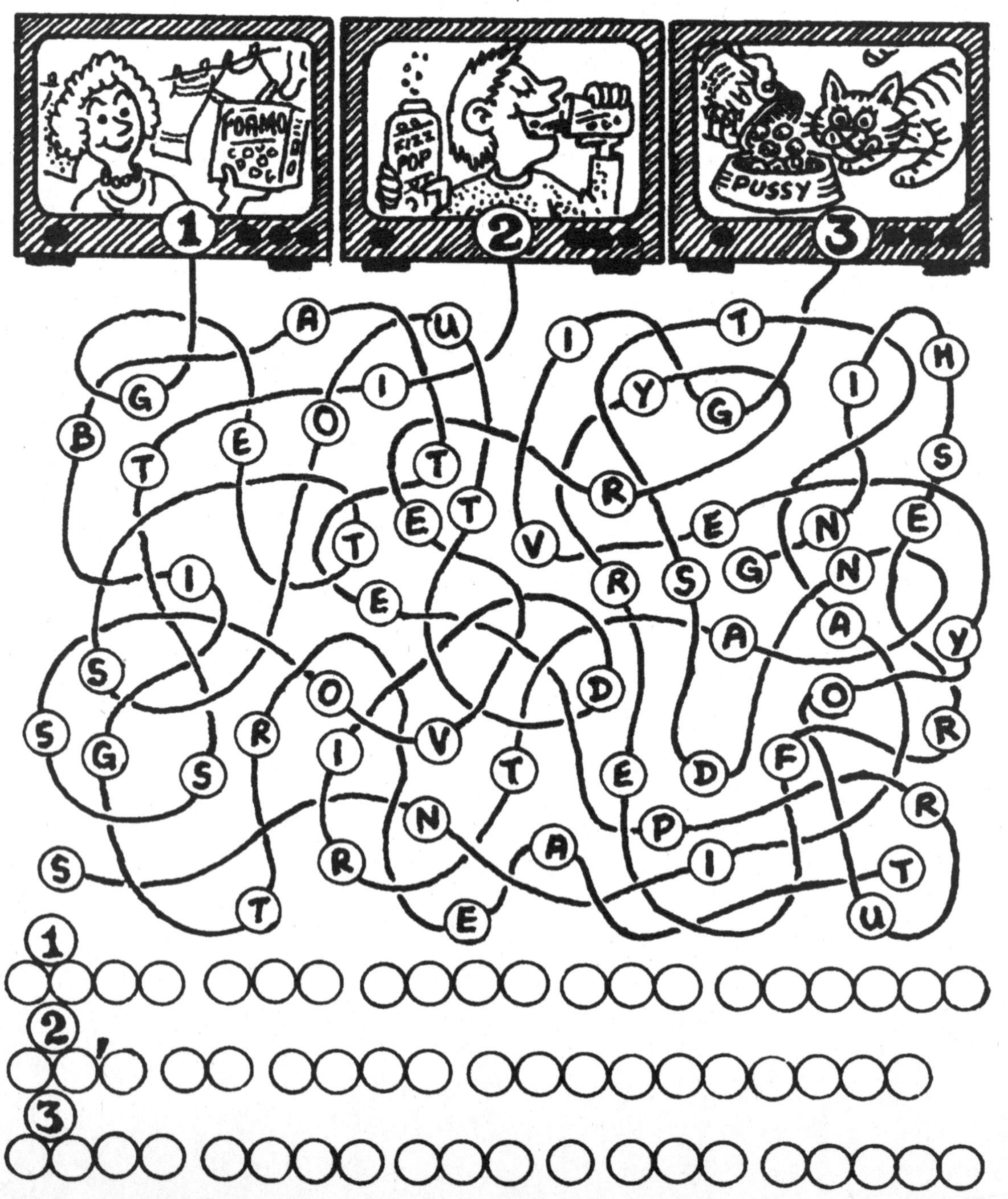

154

Spiral Puzzle

Fit the answers into the grid—the last letter of one answer is the first of the next. Then write the letters in the shaded circles in the squares below to spell out the answer to this joke: **What's big, white, and fluffy and beats its chest?**

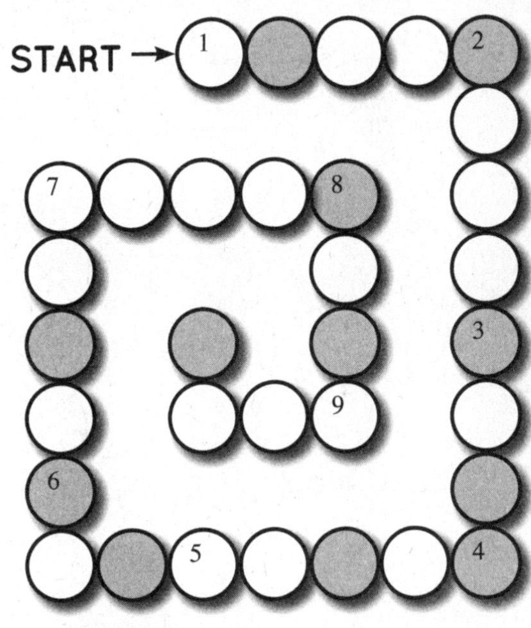

CLUES

1 Fumes from burning (5)
2 Very keen (5)
3 Water droplets falling from the sky (4)
4 Dark period of each day (5)
5 Melody, refrain (4)
6 Exactly the same (5)
7 Smallest amount (5)
8 Group of players (4)
9 Not generous; unkind (4)

Punch line: A □□□□□□□□–□□□□!

155

ACROSS

3 Stupid people (7)
5 Move on snow (3)
6 At the back (3)
8 Inn (6)

DOWN

1 Pails (7)
2 Aussie bird (3)
4 Exertion of physical or mental power (6)
7 Night before (3)

156

Egg Timer

To answer these clues, you have to remove a letter from the previous answer and (if necessary) rearrange the letters to get the new answer. When you pass clue 5, you have to do the opposite—add a letter each time. We have put the first one in to start you off.

~~1 Car windshield de-icer~~
2 Scratch
3 Prank
4 Cloak
5 Peaked hat
6 Speed
7 Soft-skinned fruit
8 Deliver a sermon
9 Less expensive

157

ACROSS
2 Hits hard (4)
4 Sea bird (4)
5 Egg-shaped (4)
6 Hindu woman's dress (4)
7 Trim (4)
8 Pealed (4)

DOWN
1 Dried grape (7)
2 Expelling air (7)
3 Squares surrounded by buildings (7)

158

Picture This

Write the name of each item pictured into the grid, then transfer the letters to the coded boxes in the lower grid. If you do this correctly, you will reveal what the mother is singing to her baby.

159

Crossword

Solve the crossword the usual way. When you have finished, rearrange the letters in the shaded squares to find out what sledders shout to encourage their dogs to go faster!

ACROSS

1 Nocturnal flying animal (3)
2 White greasy part of meat (3)
5 Long-necked animal (7)
6 Comparable, alike (7)
8 Writing tool (3)
9 Except for, apart from (3)

DOWN

1 Loud firework noise (4)
3 Narrative, story (4)
4 Look at carefully (7)
6 Large boat for sea travel (4)
7 Underground part of a plant (4)

1				2		3
			4			
5						
6						7
8				9		

__ __ __ __ **is what sledders shout to encourage their husky dogs to make them pull the sled faster.**

160

Break Out

If you cross out any letter that appears more than once in the grid, then rearrange the remaining letters, you'll reveal the punch line to this joke: *If you live in an igloo, what's the worst thing about global warming?*

O	M	I	U	G
U	T	E	B	R
E	P	Y	Z	A
V	G	B	C	M
B	N	T	E	Z

Kriss Kross

Solve the kriss kross by filling in all the words related to bad weather. Start with the 8-letter word, BLUSTERY. When you've finished, rearrange the letters in the shaded squares to spell another type of stormy weather with driving snow, strong winds, and intense cold.

4 Letters
GALE
GASP
HOWL
PANT
PUFF
ROAR

6 Letters
BREATH
BREEZE
STORMY
ZEPHYR

7 Letters
CYCLONE
TEMPEST
TYPHOON

8 Letters
BLUSTERY

9 Letters
TURBULENT
WINDSWEPT

The other type of stormy weather is a:

__________!

162

1		2		3		4		■
	■		■		■		■	5
6			■	7				
	■		■		■	■	■	
8				■	9	10		
	■	■	■	11	■		■	
12		13			■	14		
	■		■		■		■	
■	15							

ACROSS

1 Paper-cutting tool (8)
6 Organ of sight (3)
7 Instrument receiving sound programs (5)
8 Silence, quiet (4)
9 Move around (4)
12 Lift up, elevate (5)
14 Body of salt water (3)
15 Bones that make up a body (8)

DOWN

1 German ____, Alsatian dog (8)
2 Thoughts, plans (5)
3 Without doubt (4)
4 Little ____ Riding Hood, story (3)
5 Water-spraying ornament (in a pond) (8)
10 Troubled, worried (5)
11 Door chime (4)
13 Dark-colored liquid used for writing and printing (3)

163

Word Link

Starting at the top left, fit the names of the objects into the diagram so that the last letter of one word is the first letter of the next. But watch out, the pictures are not in order.

164
Giant Kriss Kross

Solve the kriss kross by filling in all the words related to archaeology. When you've finished, rearrange the letters in the shaded squares to spell out the punch line to the joke under the grid.

7 Letters
HISTORY
PYRAMID
RAMPART
UNEARTH

4 Letters
COIN
DATE
FIND
RUIN
RUNE
TOMB

5 Letters
HOARD
RELIC
SPEAR

6 Letters
BROOCH
EXPERT
FOSSIL
MOSAIC

11 Letters
ARCHAEOLOGY
STONE CIRCLE

12 Letters
BURIAL GROUND
CARBON DATING

8 Letters
DISCOVER
EXCAVATE
MONOLITH
TREASURE
BATTLE-AX

9 Letters
ANTIQUITY
ARROWHEAD

Why was the Egyptian kid confused?

_ _ _ _ _ _ _ _ _ _   _ _ _ _   _ _ _ _ _ _ _ _

_ _ _ _   _ _   _ _ _ _ _ _ _ _!

Solutions

1

2

3

ACROSS: **5** Chest **8** Primeval **9** Cream **10** Turnpike **11** Sport **14** Arm **16** Carpet **17** Aspect **18** End **20** Fiery **24** Sterling **25** Tonic **26** Geronimo **27** Adage

DOWN: **1** Spite **2** Diary **3** Tempo **4** Banker **6** Hornpipe **7** Shamrock **12** Marigold **13** Sparring **14** Ate **15** Mad **19** Netted **21** Brook **22** Mimic **23** Aglow

4

5

6

7

8

9

10

11

12

13

J	N	E	P	T	X	L	G	C	Z	O	A	F
I	V	W	M	Q	D	U	Y	K	B	H	S	R

14

"Not everything that can be counted counts, and not everything that counts can be counted." Albert Einstein (1879–1955)

15

B	U	R	G	U	N	D	Y
M	A	N	D	A	R	I	N
D	A	F	F	O	D	I	L
B	I	N	D	W	E	E	D
B	I	L	B	E	R	R	Y
B	R	O	C	C	O	L	I
W	I	S	T	E	R	I	A

16

The boy scout is going **CAMPING**.

17

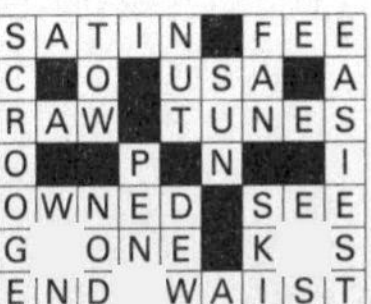

18

1 Crowd
2 Short
3 Swing
4 Still
5 Scare
The country is **CHILE**.

19

20

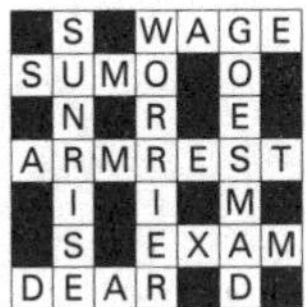

21

22

23

C	U	P
P	U	P
P	O	P
P	O	T

24

The boat is a **TRAWLER**.

25

1 Carrot
2 Ballet
3 Jungle
4 Ice cream
5 Coffee
6 Boulder
7 Emerald
8 Donald
9 Kitten
10 Balloon
The hidden word is **CALIFORNIA**.

26

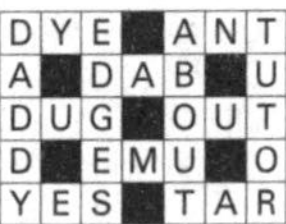

27

1 Praise/Emerge
2 Grotto/Outlaw
3 Boring/Ground
4 Revise/Expert
5 Caress/Scored
6 Carton/Nature
7 Phobia/Actual
8 Carpet/Teased
We have been transported to the **STONE AGE**.

28

29

1 Factory **2** Yeast **3** Table tennis **4** Salt Lake City **5** Yale **6** Ellis **7** Studio **8** *Out of Africa* **9** Aliens **10** Shortcut **11** Tissues **12** Seconds **13** Smooth **14** Haggis **15** Sights **16** Shop **17** Pea **18** Alp

The two instruments are **FLUGELHORN** and **SOUSAPHONE**.

30

From top to bottom: try, price, erasers, daughters, blacksmiths, boomerang, Austria, outer, bee

The dog is an **IRISH SETTER.**

31

P	I	E
P	I	T
P	A	T
H	A	T

32

1 Knight/night
2 Easter/tears
3 Cavern/crane
4 Videos/doves
5 Kennel/kneel
6 Desert/trees
7 Cousin/coins
8 Nerves/seven
9 Aerial/Ariel
10 Fasten/feast
11 Mother/Homer

The famous basketball player is **KEVIN DURANT**.

33

34

The snack is a **SANDWICH**.

35

36

37

38

There was a young
lady called Grace
Who fancied a trip
into space,
To head for the stars
Maybe Venus or Mars,
Would sure put a smile
on her face.

39

1 Coin
2 Nail
3 Nick
4 Onion
5 Post
6 Sage
7 Silk
8 Stage
9 Stew
10 You

The fact is **AN OKAPI'S TONGUE IS SO LONG IT CAN LICK ITS OWN EYES.**

40

H	W	J	Q	A	V	K	U	C	F	P	M	D
X	I	Y	R	B	L	S	G	T	N	Z	E	O

41

1 Parrot
2 Even
3 Tomato
4 East
5 Rabbit
6 Panda
7 Ajar
8 Neighbors

The book is ***PETER PAN*** by **J. M. BARRIE**.

42

R	E	D
T	E	D
T	E	N
T	A	N

43

The missing ingredient is **BAT WING**.

44

Ladder one:
WARM, WORM, FORM, FORT, FOOT, FOOL, COOL

Ladder two:
BALL, BILL, SILL, SILK, SINK, LINK, LINE

45

1 Mango
2 Anvil
3 Grass
4 Arrow
5 Zebra
6 Index
7 Niece
8 Error
The hidden word is **MAGAZINE**.

46

47

48

1 Wide **2** Wade **3** Wave **4** Wake
5 Bake **6** Cake **7** Case **8** Cash
9 Mash **10** Wash **11** Wish **12** Wise

49

B	O	Y
B	A	Y
M	A	Y
M	A	N

50

51

BEN – The Greek Islands
LIZ – An African safari
IAN – Trip to Disneyland

52

53

54

55

L	I	G	H	T	S
T	I	N	S	E	L
S	W	E	E	T	S
B	A	U	B	L	E
I	C	I	C	L	E
A	N	G	E	L	S

56

57

The other indoor game is **TWISTER**!

58

59

60

Sam has forgotten her **GYM KIT**.

61

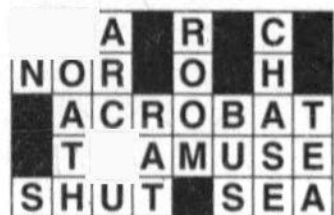

62

63

64

A Rubble
B Vincent
C William
D Tawny
E Hatter
F Hoot
G Hour
H Steed
I Wash
J Track

The prehistoric pun is: **WHY WAS THE ROCK BRAVER THAN THE MOUNTAIN? IT WAS A LITTLE BOULDER!**

65

The weather forecast is **SHOWERY.**

66

67

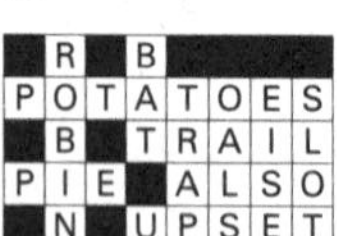

68

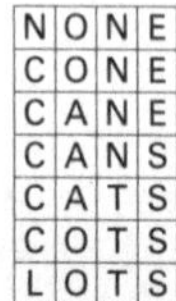

69

What two countries should the chef use when he's making Christmas dinner?
TURKEY and **GREECE.**

70

ACROSS: 1 Crowd **6** Adder **7** Diver **8** Wept **10** Arch **13** Limes **14** Twice **16** Wasps
DOWN: 2 Raise **3** Dark **4** Udder **5** Trash **8** White **9** Paris **11** Cheap **12** Flew

71

1 Colder
2 Older
3 Rode
4 Rod
5 Or
6 Row
7 Wore
8 Worse
9 Shower

72

73

MOT HER BAL

TEN DON ATE

74

Ladder one:
GALL, FALL, FAIL, FOIL, FOOL, FOOD, WOOD

Ladder two:
MAIN, LAIN, LOIN, LOON, LOOM, DOOM, DOOR

75

1 Obama
2 Build
3 Sword
4 Theft
5 Abbot
6 Chess
7 Lemon
8 Error
The hidden word is **OBSTACLE.**

76

77

1 Banana skin
2 Grease
3 Fish
4 Ice
5 Oil
6 Moss
7 Soap
8 Mud

78

79

1 Charming
2 Amazement
3 Tallness
4 Flautist

The edible word is **HAZELNUT.**

80

The missing words, in order, are **COAT, ANORAK, HOOD, SCARF, SWEATER, HAT, GLOVES, MITTS, SUITS, BOOTS, SOCKS, HEATING.**

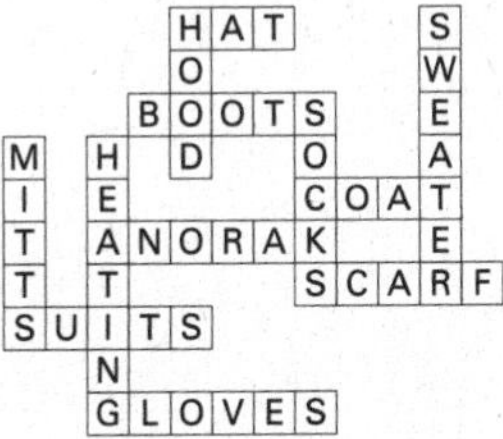

81

1 Dart **2** Bart **3** Bark **4** Park **5** Pack
6 Pick **7** Kick **8** Mick **9** Mice **10** Dice
11 Dire **12** Dirt

82

D	E	N
E	Y	E
N	E	T

83

84

85

1 Clue **2** Chew **3** Coo
4 Owe **5** Mow **6** Toe
7 Gym **8** Dim **9** Jim
10 Orb **11** Daub **12** Absorb
13 Canoe **14** Lasso **15** Argue
16 Weight **17** Kate **18** Bait

The style of trousers is **COMBAT.**

86

1 Shears
2 Norway
3 Bright
The insect is an **EARWIG.**

87

S	C	Y	T	H	E
K	E	T	T	L	E
E	R	A	S	E	R
G	O	L	F	E	R
N	O	T	I	C	E
E	L	E	V	E	N
S	H	R	I	M	P
S	P	I	D	E	R

The saying is: **A STITCH IN TIME SAVES NINE!**

88

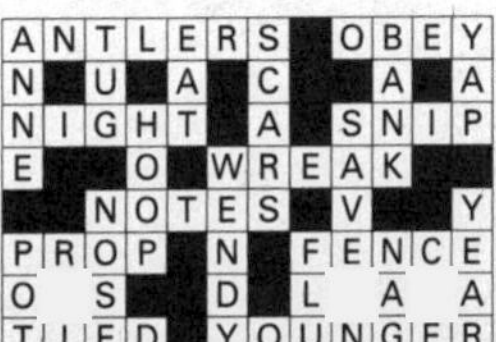

89

1 Bucket
2 Crown
3 Branch
4 Eyes
5 Gloves
6 Donkey

The item of stationery you could use to draw is **CRAYON**.

90

The six completed words are: MinCer, deAn, baNker, Clean, Award, priNce.

The six added letters spell out the word **CANCAN**.

91

C	A	M	E	R	A
P	H	O	T	O	S
T	R	I	P	O	D
L	E	N	S	E	S
M	E	M	O	R	Y
P	R	I	N	T	S

92

M	U	T	E
U	S	E	R
T	E	A	R
E	R	R	S

93

94

1 Jaguar
2 Frog
3 Whale
4 Magpie
5 Hyena
6 Fir
7 Parrot
8 Turtle
9 Tiger
10 Kitten

The fruit is a **GRAPEFRUIT.**

95

B	A	D
B	E	D
B	E	G
L	E	G

96

97

98

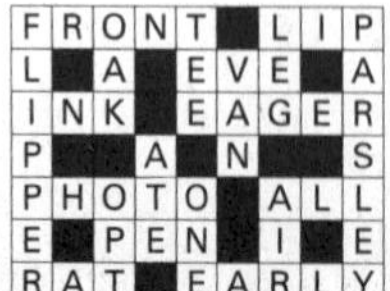

99

100

101

The color is **BROWN**.

102

1 Goose
2 Mouse
3 Score
4 Guide
The item is a **DRESS**.

103

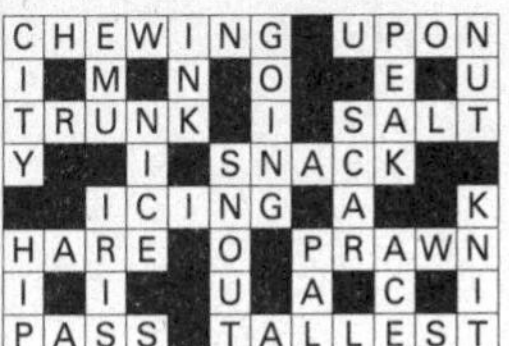

104

105

C	A	L	L
H	A	L	L
B	A	L	L
T	A	L	L
T	E	L	L

106

1 Start/Star
2 March/Cram
3 Shout/Shot
4 Exams/Axes
5 Petal/Tale
6 Sweet/West
7 Large/Gale

The rabbit is **THUMPER**.

107

1 Tomato
2 Batter
3 Stereo
4 School
5 Hornet

The mountain is **MATTERHORN**. (The Matterhorn is the Mountain of Mountains. Shaped like a jagged tooth, it's a magnet for adventurers looking for a mythical climb in Switzerland.)

108

C	M	L	K	A	S	Q	B	E	R	O	H	Y
G	U	W	N	V	D	T	P	J	Z	I	F	X

109

Ladder one:
SOUP, SOUL, FOUL, FOOL, COOL, COWL, BOWL

Ladder two:
LEFT, DEFT, DAFT, DART, HART, HARD, HAND

110

1 Raven
2 Igloo
3 Crown
4 Opium
5 Crumb
6 House
7 Empty
8 Trout

The hidden word is **RICOCHET**.

111

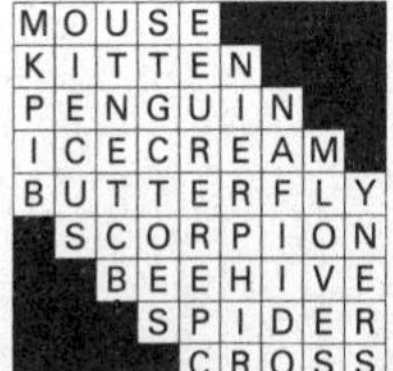

The Christmas dessert is **MINCE PIES**.

112

1 Emerald
2 Dawn
3 Night
4 Triangle
5 Eagle
6 Examination
7 Nearly
8 Year
9 Rainbow

113

114

1 Aid
2 Aunt
3 Boa
4 Eight
5 Fur
6 Jacket
7 Morn
8 None
9 Pony

The fact is: **A KANGAROO CAN JUMP THIRTY FEET IN ONE BOUND.**

115

The words in order are **LUNCH, RESTAURANT, EAT, MENU, PRICE, TRAY, DRINK, PAY, FORKS, TABLE, FOOD, WAITER, BILL.**

116

The words in order are **COW, WALRUS, STORK, KANGAROO, OSTRICH, HEN, NET, THISTLE, EEL, LAMB, BUTTERFLY, YACHT.**

117

118

119

120

T	E	A	M
E	L	S	E
A	S	K	S
M	E	S	S

121

122

123

The plant is a **THISTLE.**

124

1 Tissue **2** Shoe **3** Lasso **4** You
5 Glue **6** True **7** Lynx **8** Sphinx
9 Rinks **10** Dyes **11** Guys **12** Lies
13 Freeze **14** Seize **15** Peas **16** Mate
17 Bait **18** Eight

The hidden word is **SUNSET.**

125

1 Honest
2 Rivals
3 Medals

The state is **NEVADA.**

126

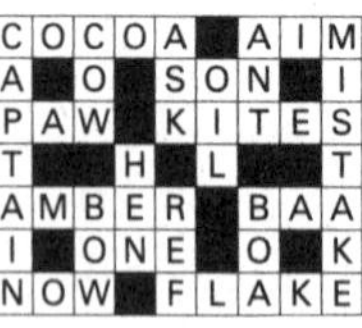

127

ACROSS 1 Moon, apple, pig, lamp, egg = MAPLE **4** Hat, anchor, seven, table, envelope = HASTE **5** Horn, owl, two, eight, ladder = HOTEL
DOWN 1 Moon, octopus, tree, hat, shell = MOTHS **2** Pig, rake, ear, seven, elephant, nine, two = PRESENT **3** Matches, envelope, tent, airplane, ladder = METAL

128

1 Disc **2** Fish **3** Kate **4** Roar
5 Near **6** Taxi **7** Mate **8** Cats

The fruit is **CHERRIES.**

129

1 Femur
2 Arrow
3 Bruno
4 April
5 Ghost

The word is **FRUIT.**

130

131

132

133

GER	MAN	NER
GAR	AGE	NDA

134

135

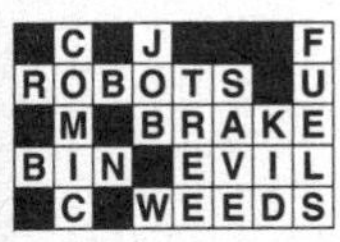

136

1 Flame
2 Fireplace
3 Ashes
4 Burning
5 Blazing
6 Heater
7 Bonfire
8 Smoke

137

The famous dog is **SNOOPY**. His owner is Charlie Brown from the *Peanuts* cartoon.

138

COLD
COLT
COAT
MOAT
MEAT
HEAT

139

140

1 He makes sure all your lights work.
2 She books your holidays.
3 He sells salmon and trout.

141

The other type of bread is **PITA**.

142

1 Poison
2 Castle
3 Kitten
4 Banana
5 Baboon
6 Flower
7 Carrot
8 Cowboy
9 Hammer

The word is **SNOWSTORM**.

143

144

WET
BET
BAT
BAY
DAY
DRY

145

Hammer, Easing, Attack, Dragon, Lizard, Effort, String, Sunday, Hiccup, Oxygen, Record, Shiver, Escape, Magpie, Action, Needle

The ghost is the **HEADLESS HORSEMAN.**

146

	S		C	O	D	E
B	U	S	H		E	
	R		A	R	C	H
	G		S		A	
J	E	D	I		M	
	O		N	I	P	S
S	N	A	G		S	

147

JAGUAR
COUGAR
SPHYNX
BENGAL
MOGGIE
BOMBAY

148

149

150

151

1 Steps
2 Stick
3 Grape
4 Small
5 Track

The word is **STALK**.

152

153

1 Gets out dirt and stains.
2 It's so very refreshing.
3 Give your pet a big treat.

154

1 Smoke
2 Eager
3 Rain
4 Night
5 Tune
6 Equal
7 Least
8 Team
9 Mean

What's big, white, and fluffy and beats its chest?
A **MERINGUE-UTAN**!

155

156

1 Scraper
2 Scrape
3 Caper
4 Cape
5 Cap
6 Pace
7 Peach
8 Preach
9 Cheaper

157

158

The mother is singing a **LULLABY**.

159

MUSH is what sledders shout to encourage their husky dogs to pull the sled faster.

160

If you live in an igloo, what's the worst thing about global warming?
NO PRIVACY.

161

The other type of stormy weather is a **BLIZZARD**.

162

163

164

Why was the Egyptian kid confused?
BECAUSE HIS DADDY WAS A MUMMY!

COLLECT
THESE
FUN BOOKS
IN THE
GO FUN!
SERIES